Liturgies of the Early Catholic Church

Liturgies of the Early Catholic Church

Liturgies of the Early Catholic Church

© Lighthouse Publishing 2025

Written by: St. James (AD ? to AD 44)
Written by: St. Mark (AD 12 to AD 86)
Translated by: George Ross Merry B.A (1841-1930)
Translated by: James Donaldson LL.D (1831-1915)
Updated into Modern U.S English: A.M. Overett B.A, REL. (b.1960)

All rights reserved. Without limiting the rights under copyright reserved above, no part of this publication may be reproduced, stored in a retrieval system, or transmitted, in any form or by any means (electronic, mechanical, photocopying, recording or otherwise), without the prior written permission of the copyright owner of this book.

Published by
Lighthouse Publishing
SAN 257-4330
228 Freedom Parkway
Hoschton, GA 30548
United States of America

www.lighthousechristianpublishing.com

Introductory Notice to the Early Liturgies.

It is in curious contrast with the work of Brett and others like-minded that we have in these Edinburgh translations a reflection from the minds of divines who are unused to liturgies, and who have no interest in their elucidation. For the mere reader this is not an advantage; but the student who goes to the originals will find that it affords at times no inconsiderable help. These translations are "inartificially drawn," as the lawyers say. They are so much Greek and Latin rendered grammatically by competent scholars, who have no theories to sustain, and who are equally devoid of *technique* and of a disposition to exhibit it for the support of preconceptions. Not infrequently one gets a new view of certain stereotyped expressions from the way in which they are here handled. The liturgiologist finds his researches freshened by etymologies he had hardly thought of, here literally rendered. Of course, these are mere specimens, and no one can use them for argument, except by comparison with the Greek, or the Latin of Renaudot, or the originals in Syriac or Coptic; but they will prove very useful in many ways. The whole science is in its infancy; and we have no specimen of a primitive liturgy unless it be the Clementine, so called. The specimens here given are like cloth of gold (Ps. xlv. 13), moth-eaten and patched, and spangled over with tinsel; and the true artist has only the one object in view,—to restore it, that is, to the king's daughter, as it was aforetime.

The following is the announcement of the Messrs. Clark in the Edinburgh edition: "The Liturgy of St. James has been translated by William Macdonald, M.A.; that of the Evangelist Mark by George Ross Merry, B.A.; and that of the Holy Apostles by Dr. Donaldson."

It will be observed that the translations are given in the Edinburgh series with hardly a line of comment, and with no editorial helps to the reader whatever. These have been scantily supplied, here and there, where the case seemed to require some elucidation; and in a few instances I have ventured to reduce a word or two in the rendering to liturgical phraseology.

The interest which has recently been awakened in *liturgiology*, and which exists among the learned so generally, will justify me in stating somewhat at large the considerations which are prerequisites to an intelligent study of these compilations. I shall not depart from my rule, nor formulate my personal convictions; but I must indicate sources of information not mentioned by the Edinburgh editors, only remarking, that, while they have cited the learned and excellent Dr. Neale, with others who advance untenable claims in some instances, I shall refer to writers of a more moderate school, such as have taken a less narrow and more historic view of the whole matter. By claiming too much, and by reading their own ideas back into the ancient exemplars, many good and learned men have overdone their argument, and confused scriptural simplicity with the artificial systems of post-Nicene ages. Earnest and worthy of respect as they are, I must therefore prefer a class of writers who breathe the spirit of the ante-Nicene Fathers as better elucidating the primitive epoch and its principles, alike in doctrine and worship.

Hippolytus, in a few terse sentences, has pointed out the epoch of David, in its vast import, as the dawning of Christianity itself. More elaborately, a recent writer of great erudition has expounded the same historic fact, and given us the pivot of Hebrew history on which turns the whole system of that "goodly fellowship of prophets" who heralded the Sun of righteousness as successive constellations rise before the day. The learned Dean Payne-Smith, more minutely than Hippolytus, identifies Samuel, the master of David, as the great instrument of God in shaping the institutions of Moses to be a prelude to the Advent; in other words, transforming a local and tribal religion into that of Catholicity. The value of the Dean's condensed and luminous elaboration of this cardinal truth can hardly be overstated.

But, to go behind even the Dean's stand-point, we shall better comprehend the era of which, under God, Samuel was the author, by noting the immense importance of that specific Mosaic ordinance which not only made it possible, but which proves that an all-wise *prolepsis* governed the whole law of Moses. We generally conceive of the Mosaic system as one of unlimited hecatombs and burnt-offerings. On the contrary, it was a system restricting and limiting the unsystematized primeval institution of sacrifice, which had done its work by passing into the universal religions and rituals of Gentilism. When the seminal idea of expiation, atonement, and the blood of innocence as a propitiation for guilt, was communicated to all the families of the earth, the Mosaic institutions limited sacrifices for the faithful, and localized them with marvelous significance. Previously the faithful everywhere had imitated the sacrifices of their fathers, Noah and Abraham, who reared their altars everywhere, as Job also did,—wherever they dwelt or sojourned. Now mark the first step towards a more spiritual worship, based, nevertheless, on the fundamental principle of sacrifice. Moses ordains as follows:—

1. "When ye go over Jordan, and dwell in the land which the Lord your God giveth you, then *there shall be a place* which the Lord your God shall choose to cause His name to dwell there; *thither shall ye bring all that I command you*, your burnt-offerings," etc.

2. "Take heed to thyself that thou offer not thy burnt-offerings in every place that thou sees; but *in the place which the Lord shall choose* in one of the tribes, *there* thou shalt offer thy burnt-offerings, and there thou shalt do all that I command thee."

3. "If the place which the Lord thy God hath chosen to put His name there, be too far from thee" [i.e., *for frequent sacrifices; observe, nevertheless, the law as to the sanctity of blood in thy common use of meats, and forbear to sacrifice, till the opportunity comes*], "only thy *holy things* which thou hast, and thy vows, thou shalt take, and *go unto the place which the Lord shall choose*; and thou shalt offer thy burnt-offerings, the flesh and the blood, upon the altar of the Lord thy God."

4. "Three times in a year shall all thy males appear before the Lord thy God, *in the place which He shall choose*."

5. "Thou may not sacrifice The Passover within any of thy gates; but *at the place which the Lord thy God shall choose* to place His name in, *there thou shalt sacrifice the Passover.*"

Note, further, that all this provision and *pre*vision was part of the great Messianic system, which reached its crisis in the time of David, as prophetic of "the Son of David."

It was the office of Samuel to take the Mosaic ordinances just there, and to shape them for the advent of the Lamb of God, for His sacrifice upon Calvary, and for the setting-up of His universal kingdom.

The Institutions of Samuel, therefore, were *in essence* institutions for the Gospel-day, and they were completed by the anointing of David as king, and by his prophetic mission to provide the Psalter (of which more, by and by); then the Ark came out of curtains, and the Lord chose and appointed *the place* of which Moses had spoken,—none other than the spot where Abraham had rehearsed in type the Sacrifice and Resurrection of Christ, according as it was written:8 "Jehovah-Jireh…*in the mount of the Lord* it shall be seen." Thus, all sacrifice acceptable to God was shown to have reference to the Paschal Lamb, who on that mount of the Lord should be sacrificed, and rise again, as was accomplished in a figure aforetime.

And next, the Psalmist commemorates the putting away of the migratory Tabernacle, and the *rest* of the Ark of the Covenant in the place designed for the grand accomplishment of redemption ("the sure mercies of David"), as follows:—

"He refused the tabernacle of Joseph, and chose not the tribe of Ephraim: but chose the tribe of Judah, *the Mount Zion* which He loved. And He built His sanctuary like high palaces, like the earth which He hath established forever."

Thus, localized sacrifice was made to designate *the spot* where the one propitiatory sacrifice should be

offered, "for the sins of the whole world;" and that spot in turn interpreted the great canon of redemption,—
"Without shedding of blood is no remission:"

And all this, being accomplished in the Messiah, passed away forever. The veil of the Temple was rent when Jesus cried, "It is finished."
And now let us note the "Institutions of Samuel." The localizing of the Temple-worship made way for the clearer revelation of spiritual sacrifices: the Temple itself was to be supplied with an expository liturgy. Moreover, a liturgical system, revolving about the central worship of the Temple, was to be brought to every man's door by the establishment of the synagogue for the villages of Israel. The synagogue-worship became, therefore, the education and preparation of the faithful for the simple and spiritual worship of the new law. This our Lord Himself expounded in the grand Catholicity of His words to the outcast Samaritans:—

"The hour cometh, when ye shall neither in this mountain, nor yet at Jerusalem, worship the Father....But the hour cometh, and now is, when the true worshippers shall worship the Father in spirit and in truth," etc.

We have seen that the hour promised by Malachi was supposed by the Ante-Nicene Fathers to be here intended: "My name shall be great among the Gentiles; and *in every place* incense shall be offered unto My name, and a pure offering."
The student of this series must have observed that the primitive writers were universally impressed with these principles, and they are essential to the study of the

liturgies here introduced into the series by the Edinburgh editors. For other purposes, expounding the prophetic system, on a text of St. Peter, Dean Payne-Smith has incidentally elucidated these ideas so fully, and with such originality, that I leave the student to consult his pages, with only the following important hints to those who may fail to see them:—

1. We find the prophet Samuel instituting "Schools of the Prophets," out of which grew the synagogue system supplying the rabbinical education to Israel, and furnishing chiefs to the synagogues. See Acts iii. 24; and compare 1 Sam. x. 5, xix. 20, and 1 Chron. ix. 22.

2. We find the institution of choral worship and the chanting of hymns—e.g., of Moses and Miriam, and Hannah (Samuel's mother)—in full operation under Samuel.

3. We find David at this juncture inspired, as "the sweet singer of Israel," to supply the Psalter, which in divers arrangements has continued among Christians to be the marrow of public worship "in every place," and throughout the world.

4. The reading of the law and the prophets was now set in order; and not only was the Temple supplied with teachers, but also the villages in every tribe.

5. Thus the Christian Church was provided with a system of worship from the hour of its institution, the synaxis succeeding the synagogue; the "ministration of the word" being enriched by Gospels and Epistles, by psalms and hymns and spiritual songs, and by "the prayers" (based upon the *Shemone esre*) which now began to be composed and multiplied in the churches. Touching "free prayer" as exemplified in the first ages, see St.

Cyprian's *Epistles* more especially: "Let us pray for the lapsed," etc.

6. It is most significant, that, as St. Paul was not present at the institution of the Lord's Supper, he was, nevertheless, "not behind the chiefest of the Apostles," even in this. He also "received" the whole knowledge of the institution, and became, in so far, the author of an original Gospel in his details of Christ's great oblation of Himself. Hereupon, he adds the sacrificial expositions of the Epistle to the Hebrews, and "delivered the ordinances" to *every church* (κατὰ τάξιν), providing for order and decorum in divine offices.

This he seems to have done as "Liturge" and "Hierurge," or evangelical priest, *"ministering in sacrifice the Gospel of God,"* etc.

Compare, then, with the Scriptures, Justin Martyr's account of the early worship of Christians; and after consulting the (so-called) "Clementine Liturgy," the student will be qualified to form an enlightened judgment upon the primitive and the interpolated elements of the following liturgies. For we must bear in mind that they are reflected from mss., not one of which has any claim to represent the *Ante-Nicene* period. To purify them, therefore, by Scripture, and the truly primitive testimonies of this series, is a task yet remaining to be accomplished, and one which may well invoke the most conscientious and patient labors of the most learned in the land.

Here follows the Edinburgh Introductory Notice:—

The word *Liturgy* has a special meaning as applied to the following documents. It denotes the service used in the celebration of the Eucharist.

Various liturgies have come down to us from antiquity; and their age, authorship, and genuineness have been matter of keen discussion. In our own country two writers on this subject stand specially prominent: the Rev. William Palmer, M.A., who in his *Origines Liturgicæ* gave a dissertation on Primitive Liturgies; and the Rev. J. Mason Neale, who devoted a large portion of his life to liturgies, edited four of them in his *Tetralogia Liturgica*, five of them in his *Liturgies of St. Mark, St. James, St. Clement, St. Chrysostom, and St. Basil*, and discussed them in a masterly manner in several works, but especially in his *General Introduction to a History of the Holy Eastern Church* Ancient liturgies are generally divided into four families,—the Liturgy of the Jerusalem Church, adopted throughout the East; the Alexandrian, used in Egypt and the neighboring countries; and the Roman and Gallican Liturgies. To these Neale has added a fifth, the Liturgy of Persia or Edessa.

There is also a liturgy not included in any of these families—the Clementine. It seems never to have been used in any public service. It forms part of the eighth book of the
Apostolical Constitutions.
The age ascribed to these documents depends very much on the temperament and inclination of the inquirer. Those who have great reverence for them think that they must have had an apostolic origin, that they contain the apostolic form, first handed down by tradition, and then committed to writing, but they allow that there is a certain amount of interpolation and addition of a date later than the Nicene Council. Such words as "consubstantial" and "mother of God" bear indisputable witness to this. Others

think that there is no real historical proof of their early existence at all,—that they all belong to a late date, and bear evident marks of having been written long after the age of the apostles.

There can scarcely be a doubt that they were not committed to writing till a comparatively late day. Those who think that their origin was apostolic allow this. "The period," says Palmer, "when liturgies were first committed to writing is uncertain, and has been the subject of some controversy. Le Brun contends that no liturgy was written till the fifth century; but his arguments seem quite insufficient to prove this, and he is accordingly opposed by Muratori and other eminent ritualists. It seems certain, on the other hand, that the liturgy of the *Apostolical Constitutions* was written at the end of the third or beginning of the fourth century; and there is no reason to deny that others may have been written about the same time, or not long after."

Neale sums up the results of his study in the following words: "I shall content myself therefore with assuming, (1) that these liturgies, though not composed by the Apostles whose names they bear, were the legitimate development of their unwritten tradition respecting the Christian Sacrifice; the words, probably, in the most important parts, the general tenor in all portions, descending unchanged from the apostolic authors. (2) That the Liturgy of St. James is of earlier date, as to its main fabric, than a.d. 200; that the Clementine Office is at least not later than 260; that the Liturgy of St. Mark is nearly coeval with that of St. James; while those of St. Basil and St. Chrysostom are to be referred respectively to the saints by whom they purport to be composed. In all these cases, several manifest insertions and additions do not alter the truth of the general statement."

1. The Roman Liturgy. The first writer who is supposed to allude to a Roman Liturgy is Innocentius, in the beginning of the fifth century; but it may well be doubted whether his words refer to any liturgy now extant. Some have attributed the authorship of the Roman Liturgy to Leo the Great, who was made bishop of Rome in a.d. 451; some to Gelasius, who was made bishop of Rome in a.d. 492; and some to Gregory the First, who was made bishop of Rome in a.d. 590. Such being the opinions of those who have given most study to the subject, we have not deemed it necessary to translate it, though Probst, in his *Liturgie der drei ersten christlichen Jahrhunderte*, probably out of affection for his own Church, has given it a place beside the Clementine and those of St. James and St. Mark.

2. The Gallican has still less claim to antiquity. In fact, Daniel marks it among the spurious. Mabillon tries to prove that three ecclesiastics had a share in the authorship of this liturgy: Musæus, presbyter of Marseilles, who died after the middle of the fifth century; Sidonius, bishop of Auvergne, who died a.d. 494; and Hilary, bishop of Poictiers, who died a.d. 366. Palmer strives to show with great ingenuity that it is not improbable that the Gallican Liturgy may have been originally derived from St. John; but his arguments are merely conjectures.

3. The Liturgy of St. James, the Liturgy of the Church of Jerusalem. Asseman, Zaccaria, Dr. Brett, Palmer, Trollope, and Neale, think that the main structure of this liturgy is the work of St. James, while they admit

that it contains some evident interpolations. Leo Allatius, Bona, Bellarmine, Baronius, and some others, think that the whole is the genuine production of the apostle. Cave, Fabricius, Dupin, Le Nourry, Basnage, Tillemont, and many others, think that it is entirely destitute of any claim to an apostolic origin, and that it belongs to a much later age.

"From the Liturgy of St. James," says Neale, "are derived, on the one hand, the forty Syro-Jacobite offices: on the other, the Cæsarean office, or Liturgy of St. Basil, with its offshoots; that of St. Chrysostom, and the Armeno-Gregorian."

There are only two manuscripts of the Greek Liturgy of St. James,—one of the tenth, the other of the twelfth century,—with fragments of a third. The first edition appeared at Rome in 1526. In more recent times it has been edited by Rev. W. Trollope, M.A., Neale in the two works mentioned above, and Daniel in his *Codex Liturgicus* Bishop Rattray edited the *Anaphora*, and attempted to separate the original from the interpolations, "though," says Neale, "the supposed restoration is unsatisfactory enough." Bunsen, in his *Analecta Ante-Nicœna*, has tried to restore the *Anaphora* to the state in which it may have been in the fourth century, "as far as was possible—quantum fieri potuit "

4. The Liturgy of St. Mark, the liturgy of the church of Alexandria. The same difference of opinion exists in regard to the age and genuineness of this liturgy as we found existing in regard to that of St. James, and the same scholars occupy the same relative position.

The offshoots from St. Mark's Liturgy are St. Basil, St. Cyril, and St. Gregory, and the Ethiopic Canon or Liturgy of All Apostles. In regard to the Liturgy of St.

Cyril, Neale says that it is "to all intents and purposes the same as that of St. Mark; and it seems highly probable that the Liturgy of St. Mark came, as we have it now, from the hands of St. Cyril, or, to use the expression of Abu'lberkat, that Cyril 'perfected' it."

There is only one manuscript of the Liturgy of St. Mark, probably belonging to the twelfth century. The first edition appeared at Paris in 1583. The liturgy is given in Renaudot's *Liturgiarum Orientalium Collectio*, tom. i. pp. 120–148, in Neale's two works, and in Daniel's *Codex Liturgicus*

5. The Liturgy of the Apostles Adæus and Maris. This liturgy has been brought prominently forward by Neale, who says: "It is generally passed over as of very inferior importance, and Renaudot alone seems to have been prepared to acknowledge in some degree its great antiquity." He thinks that it is "one of the earliest, and perhaps the very earliest, of the many formularies of the Christian Sacrifice." It is one of the three Nestorian liturgies, the other two being that of Nestorius and that of Theodore the interpreter.

A Latin translation of it is given in Renaudot's *Collectio*, which is reprinted in Daniel's *Codex Liturgicus* It is from this version that our translation is made. Several prayers and hymns are indicated only by the initial words, and the rubrical directions are probably of a much later date than the text.

The Liturgies are divided into two parts,—the part before "Lift we up our hearts," and the part after this. The first is termed the Proanaphoral Part, the second the Anaphora.

Trollope describes what he conceives to be the form of worship in the early Church, thus: "The service of this day divided itself into two parts; at the latter of which, called in the Eastern churches Liturgia mystica, and in the Western Missa fidelium, none but perfect and approved Christians were allowed to be present. To the Missa Catechumenorum, or that part of the service which preceded the prayers peculiar to communicants only, not only believers, but Gentiles, were admitted, in the hope that some might possibly become converts to the faith. After the Psalms and Lessons with which the service commenced, as on ordinary occasions, a section from the Acts of the Apostles or the Epistles was read; after which the deacon or presbyter read the Gospel. Then followed an exhortation from one or more of the presbyters; and the bishop or president delivered a *Homily* or *Sermon*, explanatory, it should seem, of the Scripture which had been read, and exciting the people to an imitation of the virtues therein exemplified. When the preacher had concluded his discourse with a doxology in praise of the Holy Trinity, a deacon made proclamation for all infidels and noncommunicants to withdraw; then came the dismissal of the several classes of catechumens, energumens, competents, and penitents, after the prayers for each respectively, as on ordinary days; and the Missa fidelium commenced. This office consisted of two parts, essentially distinct: viz., of *prayers for the faithful*, and for mankind in general, introductory to the Oblation; and the *Anaphora* or *Oblation* itself. The introductory part varied considerably in the formularies of different churches; but in the *Anaphora* all the existing liturgies so closely agree, in substance at least, if not in words, that they can only be reasonably referred to the same common origin. Their arrangement, indeed, is not always the same; but the following essential points belong, without exception, to them all:—1. The Kiss of Peace; 2. The form beginning, *Lift up your hearts*; 3. The Hymn, *Therefore with angels*, etc.; 4. Commemoration of the words of Institution; 5. The Oblation; 6. Prayer of Consecration; 7. Prayers for the Church on Earth; 8. Prayers for the Dead; 9. The Lord's Prayer; 10. Breaking of the Bread; 11. Communion."

Neale gives a more minute account of the different parts of the service. He divides the *Proanaphoral* portion into parts in the following manner:—

"Liturgy (or *Missa*) of the Catechumens.

    I. The Preparatory Prayers.

    II The Initial Hymn or Introit

    III. The Little Entrance.

    IV. The Trisagion.

    V. The Lections.

    VI. The Prayers after the Gospel, and expulsion of the Catechumen.

    1. The Prayers for the Faithful.

"Liturgy (or *Missa*) of the Faithful.

II. The Great Entrance.

III. The Offertory.

IV. The Kiss of Peace.

V. The Creed."

The *Anaphora* he divides into four parts in the following manner:—

"The great Eucharistic Prayer.   I. The Preface.

II. The Prayer of the Triumphal Hymn.

II. The Triumphal Hymn.

IV. Commemoration of Our Lord's Life.

V. Commemoration of Institution.

"The Consecration.   VI. Words of Institution of the Bread.

VII. Words of Institution of the Wine.

VIII. Introductory Prayer for the Descent of the Holy Ghost.

IX. Prayer for the Sanctification of Elements.

XI. General Intercession for Quick and Dead.

The great Intercessory Prayer.

XII. Prayer before the Lord's Prayer.

XIII. The Lord's Prayer.

XIV. The Embolismus.

The Communion.

XV. The Prayer of Inclination.

XVI. The *Holy Things for Holy Persons.*

XVII. *The Fraction.*

XVII. The Confession.

XIX. The Communion.

XX. The Antidoron: and Prayers of Thanksgiving."

The whole subject is discussed by Mr. Neale with extraordinary minuteness, fullness of detail, and perfect mastery of his subject; and to his work we refer those who wish to prosecute the study of the subject.

General Note by the American Editor.

I Have found a few less noted works most useful in my own studies, which began with Palmer's *Origines* on their first publication, followed up by *Brett*, and then by *Renaudot*. The publications of Drs. Neale and Littledale are sufficiently referred to elsewhere; and I purposely omit the mention of many purely Anglican authorities, as well as costly works from other European sources.

1. Freeman's *Principles of Divine Service*, etc. A work of incomparable utility to those who would comprehend the Jewish ritual and its preparations for Christian worship.

2. Badger's *Nestorians and their Rituals*

3. Warren's *Liturgy and Ritual of the Celtic Church*; replete with information hitherto inaccessible.

4. Scudamore's *Notitia Eucharistica*; Anglican, but full of general information.

5. Trevor's *Catholic Doctrine of Sacrifice*, etc.; a candid and learned study of this subject, and free from fanatical or visionary conceptions.

6. Hammond's *Liturgies*, etc., elsewhere spoken of.

7. Burbidge, *Liturgies and Offices,* of which I have only lately discovered the value.

8. Field's *Apostolic Liturgy and the Ep. to the Hebrews*; open to some objections, but full of valuable and suggestive information.

9. Pfaffius, Christ. Math. His invaluable *Dissertatio de Oblatione*, etc. A high Lutheran authority of great learning.

10. Marriott's *Testimony of the Catacombs*; learned and instructive.

EARLY LITURGIES.
The Divine Liturgy of James the Holy Apostle.
I.

The Priest.

I O Sovereign Lord our God, contemn me not, defiled with a multitude of sins: for, behold, I have come to this Thy divine and heavenly mystery, not as being worthy; but looking only to Thy goodness, I direct my voice to Thee: God be merciful to me, a sinner; I have sinned against Heaven, and before Thee, and am unworthy to come into the presence of this Thy holy and spiritual table, upon which Thy only-begotten Son, and our Lord Jesus Christ, is mystically set forth as a sacrifice for me, a sinner, and stained with every spot. Wherefore I present to Thee this supplication and thanksgiving, that Thy Spirit the Comforter may be sent down upon me, strengthening and fitting me for this service; and count me worthy to make known without condemnation the word, delivered from Thee by me to the people, in Christ Jesus our Lord, with whom Thou art blessed, together with Thy all holy, and good, and quickening, and consubstantial Spirit, now and ever, and to all eternity. Amen.

Prayer of the standing beside the altar.

II Glory to the Father, and to the Son, and to the Holy Spirit, the triune light of the Godhead, which is unity subsisting in trinity, divided, yet indivisible: for the

Trinity is the one God Almighty, whose glory the heavens declare, and the earth His dominion, and the sea His might, and every sentient and intellectual creature at all times proclaims His majesty: for all glory becomes Him, and honor and might, greatness and magnificence, now and ever, and to all eternity. Amen.

Prayer of the incense at the beginning.

III Sovereign Lord Jesus Christ, O Word of God, who didst freely offer Thyself a blameless sacrifice upon the cross to God even the Father, the coal of double nature, that didst touch the lips of the prophet with the tongs, and didst take away his sins, touch also the hearts of us sinners, and purify us from every stain, and present us holy beside Thy holy altar, that we may offer Thee a sacrifice of praise: and accept from us, Thy unprofitable servants, this incense as an odor of a sweet smell, and make fragrant the evil odor of our soul and body, and purify us with the sanctifying power of Thy all-holy Spirit: for Thou alone art holy, who sanctifies, and art communicated to the faithful; and glory becomes Thee, with Thy eternal Father, and Thy all-holy, and good, and quickening Spirit, now and ever, and to all eternity. Amen.

Prayer of the commencement.

IV O beneficent King eternal, and Creator of the universe, receive Thy Church, coming unto Thee through Thy Christ: fulfil to each what is profitable; lead all to perfection, and make us perfectly worthy of the grace of Thy sanctification, gathering us together within Thy holy Church, which Thou hast purchased by the precious blood of Thy only-begotten Son, and our Lord and Savior Jesus Christ, with whom Thou art blessed and glorified, together with Thy all-holy, and good, and quickening Spirit, now and ever, and to all eternity. Amen.

The Deacon.

V Let us again pray to the Lord.

The Priest, prayer of the incense at the entrance of the congregation.

God, who didst accept the gifts of Abel, the sacrifice of Noah and of Abram, the incense of Aaron and of Zacharias, accept also from the hand of us sinners this incense for an odor of a sweet smell, and for remission of our sins, and those of all Thy people; for blessed art Thou, and glory becomes Thee, the Father, and the Son, and the Holy Spirit, now and ever.

The Deacon.

Sir, pronounce the blessing.

The Priest prays.

Our Lord and God, Jesus Christ, who through exceeding goodness and love not to be restrained was crucified, and didst not refuse to be pierced by the spear and nails; who didst provide this mysterious and awful service as an everlasting memorial for us perpetually: bless Thy ministry in Christ the God, and bless our entrance, and fully complete the presentation of this our service by Thy unutterable compassion, now and ever, and to all eternity. Amen.

The responsive prayer from the Deacon.

VI. The Lord bless us, and make us worthy seraphically to offer gifts, and to sing the oft-sung hymn of the divine Trisagion, by the fullness and exceeding abundance of all the perfection of holiness, now and ever.

Then the Deacon begins to sing in the entrance.

Thou who are the only-begotten Son and Word of God, immortal; who didst submit for our salvation to become flesh of the holy God-mother, and ever-virgin Mary; who didst immutably become man and was crucified, O Christ our God, and didst by Thy death tread death underfoot; who art one of the Holy Trinity glorified together with the Father and the Holy Spirit, save us.

The Priest says this prayer from the gates to the altar.

VII God Almighty, Lord great in glory, who hast given to us an entrance into the Holy of Holies, through the sojourning among men of Thy only-begotten Son, our Lord, and God, and Savior Jesus Christ, we supplicate and invoke Thy goodness, since we are fearful and trembling when about to stand at Thy holy altar; send forth upon us, O God, Thy good grace, and sanctify our souls, and bodies, and spirits, and turn our thoughts to piety, in order that with a pure conscience we may bring unto Thee gifts, offerings, and fruits for the remission of our transgressions, and for the propitiation of all Thy people, by the grace and mercies and loving-kindness of Thy only-begotten Son, with whom Thou art blessed to all eternity. Amen.

After the approach to the altar, the Priest says:—

VIII. Peace be to all.

The People.

And to thy spirit.

The Priest.

The Lord bless us all, and sanctify us for the entrance and celebration of the divine and pure mysteries, giving rest to the blessed souls among the good and just, by His grace and loving-kindness, now and ever, and to all eternity. Amen.

Then the Deacon says the bidding prayer.

IX. In peace let us beseech the Lord.

For the peace that is from above, and for God's love to man, and for the salvation of our souls, let us beseech the Lord.

For the peace of the whole world, for the unity of all the holy churches of God, let us beseech the Lord.

For the remission of our sins, and forgiveness of our transgressions, and for our deliverance from all tribulation, wrath, danger, and distress, and from the uprising of our enemies, let us beseech the Lord.

Then the Singers sing the Trisagion Hymn.

Holy God, holy mighty, holy immortal, have mercy upon us.

Then the Priest prays, bowing.

X. O compassionate and merciful, long-suffering, and very gracious and true God, look from Thy prepared dwelling-place, and hear us Thy suppliants, and deliver us from every temptation of the devil and of man; withhold not Thy aid from us, nor bring on us chastisements too heavy for our strength: for we are unable to overcome what is opposed to us; but Thou art able, Lord, to save us from everything that is against us. Save us, O God, from the difficulties of this world, according to Thy goodness, in order that, having drawn nigh with a pure conscience to Thy holy altar, we may send up to Thee without condemnation the blessed hymn Trisagion, together with the heavenly powers, and that, having performed the service, well pleasing to Thee and divine, we may be counted worthy of eternal life.

(Aloud.)

Because Thou art holy, Lord our God, and dwells and abides in holy places, we send up the praise and the hymn Trisagion to Thee, the Father, and the Son, and the Holy Spirit, now and ever, and to all eternity.

The People.

Amen.

The Priest.

XI. Peace be to all.

The People.

And to thy spirit.

The Singers.

Alleluia.

Then there are read in order75 the holy oracles of the Old Testament, and of the prophets; and the incarnation of the Son of God is set forth, and His sufferings and resurrection from the dead, His ascension into heaven, and His second appearing with glory; and this takes place daily in the holy and divine service.

After the reading and instruction the Deacon says:—

XII. Let us all say, Lord, be merciful.

Lord Almighty, the God of our fathers;

We beseech Thee, hear us.

For the peace which is from above, and for the salvation of our souls;

Let us beseech the Lord.

For the peace of the whole world, and the unity of all the holy churches of God;

Let us beseech the Lord.

For the salvation and help of all the Christ-loving people;

We beseech Thee, hear us.

For our deliverance from all tribulation, wrath, danger, distress, from captivity, bitter death, and from our iniquities;

We beseech Thee, hear us.

For the people standing round, and waiting for the rich and plenteous mercy that is from Thee;

We beseech Thee, be merciful and gracious.

Save Thy people, O Lord, and bless Thine inheritance.

Visit Thy world in mercy and compassion.

Exalt the horn of Christians by the power of the precious and quickening cross.

We beseech Thee, most merciful Lord, hear us praying to Thee, and have mercy upon us.

The People (thrice).

Lord, have mercy upon us.

The Deacon.

XIII. For the remission of our sins, and forgiveness of our transgressions, and for our deliverance from all tribulation, wrath, danger, and distress, let us beseech the Lord.

Let us all entreat from the Lord, that we may pass the whole day, perfect, holy, peaceful, and without sin.

Let us entreat from the Lord a messenger of peace, a faithful guide, a guardian of our souls and bodies.

Let us entreat from the Lord forgiveness and remission of our sins and transgressions.

Let us entreat from the Lord the things which are good and proper for our souls, and peace for the world.

Let us entreat from the Lord, that we may spend the remaining period of our life in peace and health.

Let us entreat that the close of our lives may be Christian, without pain and without shame, and a good plea at the dread and awful judgment-seat of Christ.

The Priest.

XIV. For Thou art the gospel and the light, Savior and keeper of our souls and bodies, God, and Thy only-begotten Son, and Thy all-holy Spirit, now and ever.

The People.

Amen.

The Priest

God, who hast taught us Thy divine and saving oracles, enlighten the souls of us sinners for the comprehension of the things which have been before spoken, so that we may not only be seen to be hearers of spiritual things, but also doers of good deeds, striving after guileless faith, blameless life, and pure conversation.

(Aloud.)

In Christ Jesus our Lord, with whom Thou art blessed, together with Thy all-holy, good, and quickening Spirit, now and always, and forever.

The People.

Amen.

The Priest.

XV. Peace be to all.

The People.

And to Thy spirit.

The Deacon.

Let us bow our heads to the Lord.

The People.

To Thee, Lord.

The Priest prays, saying:—

O Sovereign giver of life, and provider of good things, who didst give to mankind the blessed hope of eternal life, our Lord Jesus Christ, count us worthy in holiness, and perfect this Thy divine service to the enjoyment of future blessedness.

(Aloud.)

So that, guarded by Thy power at all times, and led into the light of truth, we may send up the praise and the thanksgiving to Thee, the Father, the Son, and the Holy Spirit, now and ever.

The People.

Amen.

The Deacon.

XVI. Let none remain of the catechumens, none of the unbaptized, none of those who are unable to join with us in prayer. Look at one another. The door.

All erect: let us again pray to the Lord.

II

The Priest says the prayer of incense.

Sovereign Almighty, King of Glory, who knows all things before their creation, manifest Thyself to us calling upon Thee at this holy hour, and redeem us from the shame of our transgressions; cleanse our mind and our thoughts from impure desires, from worldly deceit, from all influence of the devil; and accept from the hands of us sinners this incense, as Thou didst accept the offering of Abel, and Noah, and Aaron, and Samuel, and of all Thy saints, guarding us from everything evil, and preserving us for continually pleasing, and worshipping, and glorifying Thee, the Father, and Thy only-begotten Son, and Thy all-holy Spirit, now and always, and forever.

And the Readers begin the Cherubic Hymn.

Let all mortal flesh be silent, and stand with fear and trembling, and meditate nothing earthly within itself:—

For the King of kings and Lord of lords, Christ our God, comes forward to be sacrificed, and to be given for food to the faithful; and the bands of angels go before Him with every power and dominion, the many-eyed cherubim, and the six-winged seraphim, covering their faces, and crying aloud the hymn, Alleluia, Alleluia, Alleluia.

The Priest, bringing in the holy gifts, says this prayer:—

XVII. O God, our God, who didst send forth the heavenly bread, the food of the whole world, our Lord Jesus Christ, to be a Savior, and Redeemer, and Benefactor, blessing and sanctifying us, do Thou Thyself bless this offering, and graciously receive it to Thy altar above the skies:

Remember in Thy goodness and love those who have brought it, and those for whom they have brought it, and preserve us without condemnation in the service of Thy divine mysteries: for hollowed and glorified is Thy all-honored and great name, Father, and Son, and Holy Spirit, now and ever, and to all eternity.

The Priest.
Peace be to all.
The Deacon.
Sir, pronounce the blessing.

The Priest.
Blessed be God, who blesses and sanctifies us all at the presentation of the divine and pure mysteries, and

giveth rest to the blessed souls among the holy and just, now and always, and to all eternity.

The Deacon.

XVIII Let us attend in wisdom.

The Priest begins.

I believe in one God, Father Almighty, Maker of heaven and earth, and in one Lord Jesus Christ, the Son of God: *and the rest of the Creed.*

Then he prays, bowing his neck.

XIX. God and Sovereign of all, make us, who are unworthy, worthy of this hour, lover of mankind; that being pure from all deceit and all hypocrisy, we may be united with one another by the bond of peace and love, being confirmed by the sanctification of Thy divine knowledge through Thine only-begotten Son, our Lord and Savior Jesus Christ, with whom Thou art blessed, together with Thy all-holy, and good, and quickening Spirit, now and ever, and to all eternity. Amen.

The Deacon.

XX. Let us stand well, let us stand reverently, let us stand in the fear of God, and with compunction of heart. In peace let us pray to the Lord.

The Priest.

For God of peace, mercy, love, compassion, and loving-kindness art Thou, and Thine only-begotten Son, and Thine all-holy Spirit, now and ever.

The People.
Amen.
The Priest.
Peace be to all.
The People.
And to thy spirit.
The Deacon.

Let us salute one another with a holy kiss. Let us bow our heads to the Lord.

The Priest bows, saying this prayer:—

XXI. Only Lord and merciful God, on those who are bowing their necks before Thy holy altar, and seeking the spiritual gifts that come from Thee, send forth Thy good grace; and bless us all with every spiritual blessing, that cannot be taken from us, Thou, who dwells on high, and hast regard unto things that are lowly.

(Aloud.)

For worthy of praise and worship and most glorious is Thy all-holy name, Father and Son and Holy Spirit, now and always, and to all eternity.

The Deacon.

Sir, pronounce the blessing.

The Priest.

The Lord will bless us, and minister with us all by His grace and loving-kindness.

And again.

The Lord will bless us, and make us worthy to stand at His holy altar, at all times, now and always, and forever.

And again.

Blessed be God, who blesses and sanctifies us all in our attendance upon, and service of, His pure mysteries, now and always, and forever.

The Deacon makes the Universal Litany.

XXII In peace let us pray to the Lord.

The People.

O Lord, have mercy.

The Deacon.

Save us, have mercy upon us, pity and keep us, O God, by Thy grace.

For the peace that is from above, and the loving-kindness of God, and the salvation of our souls;
Let us beseech the Lord.
For the peace of the whole world, and the unity of all the holy churches of God;
Let us beseech the Lord.
For those who bear fruit, and labor honorably in the holy churches of God; for those who remember the poor, the widows and the orphans, the strangers and needy ones; and for those who have requested us to mention them in our prayers;
Let us beseech the Lord.
For those who are in old age and infirmity, for the sick and suffering, and those who are troubled by unclean spirits, for their speedy cure from God and their salvation;
Let us beseech the Lord.
For those who are passing their days in virginity, and celibacy, and discipline, and for those in holy matrimony; and for the holy fathers and brethren agonizing in mountains, and dens, and caves of the earth;

Let us beseech the Lord.
For Christians sailing, travelling, living among strangers, and for our brethren in captivity, in exile, in prison, and in bitter slavery, their peaceful return;
Let us beseech the Lord.
For the remission of our sins, and forgiveness of our transgressions, and for our deliverance from all tribulation, wrath, danger, and constraint, and uprising against us of enemies;
Let us beseech the Lord.

For favorable weather, peaceful showers, beneficent dews, abundance of fruits, the perfect close of a good season, and for the crown of the year;

Let us beseech the Lord.

For our fathers and brethren present, and praying with us in this holy hour, and at every season, their zeal, labor, and earnestness;

Let us beseech the Lord.

For every Christian soul in tribulation and distress, and needing the mercy and succor of God; for the return of the erring, the health of the sick, the deliverance of the captives, the rest of the fathers and brethren that have fallen asleep aforetime;

Let us beseech the Lord.

For the hearing and acceptance of our prayer before God, and the sending down on us His rich mercies and compassion.

Let us beseech the Lord.

And for the offered, precious, heavenly, unutterable, pure, glorious, dread, awful, divine gifts, and the salvation of the priest who stands by and offers them;

Let us offer supplication to God the Lord.

The People.

O Lord, have mercy.

(Thrice.)

Then the Priest makes the sign of the cross on the gifts, and, standing, speaks separately thus:—

XXIII Glory to God in the highest, and on earth peace, good-will among men, etc.

(Thrice.)

Lord, Thou wilt open my lips, and my mouth shall show forth Thy praise.

(Thrice.)

Let my mouth be filled with Thy praise, O Lord, that I may tell of Thy glory, of Thy majesty, all the day.

(Thrice.)

Of the Father. Amen. And of the Son. Amen. And of the Holy Spirit. Amen. Now and always, and to all eternity. Amen.

And bowing to this side and to that, he says:

XXIV. Magnify the Lord with me, and let us exalt His name together.

And they answer, bowing:—

The Holy Ghost shall come upon thee, and the power of the Highest shall overshadow thee.

Then the Priest, at great length:—

O Sovereign Lord, who hast visited us in compassion and mercies, and hast freely given to us, Thy humble and sinful and unworthy servants, boldness to stand at Thy holy altar, and to offer to Thee this dread and bloodless sacrifice for our sins, and for the errors of the people, look upon me Thy unprofitable servant, and blot out my transgressions for Thy compassion's sake; and purify my lips and heart from all pollution of flesh and spirit; and remove from me every shameful and foolish thought, and fit me by the power of Thy all holy Spirit for this service; and receive me graciously by Thy goodness as I draw nigh to Thy altar.

And be pleased, O Lord, that these gifts brought by our hands may be acceptable, stooping to my weakness; and cast me not away from Thy presence, and abhor not my unworthiness; but pity me according to Thy great mercy, and according to the multitude of Thy mercies pass by my transgressions, that, having come before Thy glory without condemnation, I may be counted worthy of the protection of Thy only-begotten Son, and of the illumination of Thy all-holy Spirit, that I may not be as a slave of sin cast out, but as Thy servant may find grace and mercy and forgiveness of sins before Thee, both in the world that now is and in that which is to come.

I beseech Thee, Almighty Sovereign, all-powerful Lord, hear my prayer; for Thou art He who works all in all, and we all seek in all things the help and succor that come from Thee and Thy only-begotten Son, and the good and quickening and consubstantial Spirit, now and ever.

XXV. O God, who through Thy great and unspeakable love didst send forth Thy only begotten Son into the world, in order that He might turn back the lost sheep, turn not away us sinners, laying hold of Thee by this dread and bloodless sacrifice; for we trust not in our own righteousness, but in Thy good mercy, by which Thou purchases our race.

We entreat and beseech Thy goodness that it may not be for condemnation to Thy people that this mystery for salvation has been administered by us, but for remission of sins, for renewal of souls and bodies, for the well-pleasing of Thee, God and Father, in the mercy and love of Thy only-begotten Son, with whom Thou art blessed, together with Thy all-holy and good and quickening Spirit, now and always, and forever.

XXVI. O Lord God, who didst create us, and bring us into life, who hast shown to us ways to salvation, who hast granted to us a revelation of heavenly mysteries, and hast appointed us to this ministry in the power of Thy all-holy Spirit, grant, O Sovereign, that we may become servants of Thy new testament, ministers of Thy pure mysteries, and receive us as we draw near to Thy holy altar, according to the greatness of Thy mercy, that we may become worthy of offering to Thee gifts and sacrifices for our transgressions and for those of the people; and grant to us, O Lord, with all fear and a pure conscience to offer to Thee this spiritual and bloodless sacrifice, and graciously receiving it unto Thy holy and spiritual altar above the skies for an odor of a sweet spiritual smell, send down in answer on us the grace of Thy all-holy Spirit.

And, O God, look upon us, and have regard to this our reasonable service, and accept it, as Thou didst accept the gifts of Abel, the sacrifices of Noah, the priestly offices of Moses and Aaron, the peace-offerings of Samuel, the repentance of David, the incense of Zacharias.

As Thou didst accept from the hand of Thy apostles this true service, so accept also in Thy goodness from the hands of us sinners these offered gifts; and grant that our offering may be acceptable, sanctified by the Holy Spirit, as a propitiation for our transgressions and the errors of the people; and for the rest of the souls that have fallen asleep aforetime; that we also, Thy humble, sinful, and unworthy servants, being counted worthy without guile to serve Thy holy altar, may receive the reward of faithful and wise stewards, and may find grace and mercy in the terrible day of Thy just and good retribution.

Prayer of the veil.

XXVII. We thank Thee, O Lord our God, that Thou hast given us boldness for the entrance of Thy holy places, which Thou hast renewed to us as a new and living way through the veil of the flesh of Thy Christ. We therefore, being counted worthy to enter into the place of the tabernacle of Thy glory, and to be within the veil, and to behold the Holy of Holies, cast ourselves down before Thy goodness:

Lord, have mercy on us: since we are full of fear and trembling, when about to stand at Thy holy altar, and to offer this dread and bloodless sacrifice for our own sins and for the errors of the people: send forth, O God, Thy good grace, and sanctify our souls, and bodies, and spirits; and turn our thoughts to holiness, that with a pure conscience we may bring to Thee a peace-offering, the sacrifice of praise:

(Aloud.)

By the mercy and loving-kindness of Thy only-begotten Son, with whom Thou art blessed, together with Thy all-holy, and good, and quickening Spirit, now and always:

The People.

Amen.

The Priest.

Peace be to all.

The Deacon.

Let us stand reverently, let us stand in the fear of God, and with contrition: let us attend to the Holy Communion service, to offer peace to God.

The People.

The offering of peace, the sacrifice of praise.

The Priest [A veil is now withdrawn from the oblation of bread and wine.]

And, uncovering the veils that darkly invest in symbol this sacred ceremonial, do

Thou reveal it clearly to us: fill our intellectual vision with absolute light, and having purified our poverty from every pollution of flesh and spirit, make it worthy of this dread and awful approach: for Thou art an all-merciful and gracious God, and we send up the praise and the thanksgiving to Thee, Father, Son, and Holy Spirit, now, and always, and forever.

III.
The Anaphora.

Then he says aloud:—
XXVIII. The love of the Lord and Father, the grace of the Lord and Son, and the fellowship and the gift of the Holy Spirit, be with us all.
The People.
And with thy spirit.
The Priest.

Let us lift up our minds and our hearts.97
The People.
It is becoming and right.
Then the Priest prays.
Verily it is becoming and right, proper and due to praise Thee, to sing of Thee, to bless Thee, to worship Thee, to glorify Thee, to give Thee thanks, Maker of every creature visible and invisible, the treasure of eternal good things, the fountain of life and immortality, God and Lord of all:

Whom the heavens of heavens praise, and all the host of them; the sun, and the moon, and all the choir of the stars; earth, sea, and all that is in them; Jerusalem, the heavenly assembly, and church of the first-born that are written in heaven; spirits of just men and of prophets; souls of martyrs and of apostles; angels, archangels, thrones, dominions, principalities, and authorities, and dread powers; and the many-eyed cherubim, and the six-winged seraphim, which cover their faces with two wings, their feet with two, and with two they fly, crying one to another with unresting lips, with unceasing praises:

(Aloud.)

With loud voice singing the victorious hymn of Thy majestic glory, crying aloud, praising, shouting, and saying:—

The People.

Holy, holy, holy, O Lord of Sabbath, the heaven and the earth are full of Thy glory.

Hosanna in the highest; blessed is He that cometh in the name of the Lord. Hosanna in the highest.

The Priest, making the sign of the cross on the gifts, says:—

XXIX. Holy art Thou, King of eternity, and Lord and giver of all holiness; holy also Thy only-begotten Son, our Lord Jesus Christ, by whom Thou hast made all things; holy also Thy Holy Spirit, which searches all things, even Thy deep things, O God: holy art Thou, almighty, all-powerful, good, dread, merciful, most compassionate to Thy creatures; who didst make man from earth after Thine own image and likeness; who didst give him the joy of paradise; and when he transgressed Thy commandment, and fell away, didst not disregard nor desert him, O Good One, but didst chasten him as at merciful father, call him by the law, instruct him by the prophets; and afterwards didst send forth Thine only-begotten Son Himself, our Lord Jesus Christ, into the world, that He by His coming might renew and restore Thy image;

Who, having descended from heaven, and become flesh of the Holy Spirit and Virgin Godmother Mary, and having sojourned among men, fulfilled the dispensation for the salvation of our race; and being about to endure His voluntary and life-giving death by the cross, He the sinless for us the sinners, in the night in which He was betrayed, nay, rather delivered Himself up for the life and salvation of the world,

Then the Priest holds the bread in his hand, and says:—

XXX. Having taken the bread in His holy and pure and blameless and immortal hands, lifting up His eyes to heaven, and showing it to Thee, His God and Father, He gave thanks, and hallowed, and brake, and gave it to us, His disciples and apostles, saying:—

The Deacons say:

For the remission of sins and life everlasting.

Then he says aloud:—

Take, eat: this is my body, broken for you, and given for remission of sins.

The People.

Amen.

Then he takes the cup, and says:—

In like manner, after supper, He took the cup, and having mixed wine and water, lifting up His eyes to heaven, and presenting it to Thee, His God and Father, He gave thanks, and hollowed and blessed it, and filled it with the Holy Spirit, and gave it to us His disciples, saying, Drink ye all of it; this is my blood of the new testament shed for you and many, and distributed for the remission of sins.

The People.

Amen.

The Priest.

This do in remembrance of me; for as often as ye eat this bread, and drink this cup, ye do show forth the Lord's death, and confess His resurrection, till He come.

The Deacons say:—

We believe and confess:

The People.

We show forth Thy death, O Lord, and confess Thy resurrection.

The Priest (Oblation).

XXXI. Remembering, therefore, His life-giving sufferings, His saving cross, His death and His burial, and resurrection from the dead on the third day, and His ascension into heaven, and sitting at the right hand of Thee, our God and Father, and His second glorious and awful appearing, when He shall come with glory to judge the quick and the dead, and render to everyone according to His works; even we, sinful men, offer unto Thee, O Lord, this dread and bloodless sacrifice, praying that Thou wilt not deal with us after our sins, nor reward us according to our iniquities;

But that Thou, according to Thy mercy and Thy unspeakable loving-kindness, passing by and blotting out the handwriting against us Thy suppliants, wilt grant to us Thy heavenly and eternal gifts (which eye hath not seen, and ear hath not heard, and which have not entered into the heart of man) that thou hast prepared, O God, for those who love Thee; and reject not, O loving Lord, the people for my sake, or for my sin's sake:

Then he says, thrice:—

For Thy people and Thy Church supplicate Thee.

The People.

Have mercy on us, O Lord our God, Father Almighty.

Again the Priest says (Invocation):—

XXXII. Have mercy upon us, O God Almighty.

Have mercy upon us, O God our Savior.

Have mercy upon us, O God, according to Thy great mercy, and send forth on us, and on these offered gifts, Thy all-holy Spirit.

Then, bowing his neck, he says:—

The sovereign and quickening Spirit, that sits upon the throne with Thee, our God and Father, and with Thy only-begotten Son, reigning with Thee; the consubstantial104 and coeternal; that spoke in the law and in the prophets, and in Thy New Testament; that descended in the form of a dove on our Lord Jesus Christ at the river Jordan, and abode on Him; that descended on Thy apostles in the form of tongues of fire in the upper room of the holy and glorious Zion on the day of Pentecost: this Thine all-holy Spirit, send down, O Lord, upon us, and upon these offered holy gifts;

And rising up, he says aloud:—

That coming, by His holy and good and glorious appearing, He may sanctify this bread, and make it the holy body of Thy Christ.

The People.

Amen.
The Priest.
And this cup the precious blood of Thy Christ.
The People.
Amen.
The Priest by himself standing.

XXXIII. That they may be to all that partake of them for remission of sins, and for life everlasting, for the sanctification of souls and of bodies, for bearing the fruit of good works, for the stablishing of Thy Holy Catholic Church, which Thou hast founded on the Rock of Faith, that the gates of hell may not prevail against it; delivering it from all heresy and scandals, and from those who work iniquity, keeping it till the fullness of the time.

And having bowed, he says:—

XXXIV. We present them to Thee also, O Lord, for the holy places, which Thou hast glorified by the divine appearing of Thy Christ, and by the visitation of Thy all-holy Spirit; especially for the glorious Zion, the mother of all the churches; and for Thy Holy, Catholic, and Apostolic Church throughout the world: even now, O Lord, bestow upon her the rich gifts of Thy all-holy Spirit.

Remember also, O Lord, our holy fathers and brethren in it, and the bishops in all the world, who rightly divide the word of Thy truth.

Remember also, O Lord, every city and country, and those of the true faith dwelling in them, their peace and security.

Remember, O Lord, Christians sailing, travelling, sojourning in strange lands; our fathers and brethren, who are in bonds, prison, captivity, and exile; who are in mines, and under torture, and in bitter slavery. Remember, O Lord, the sick and afflicted, and those troubled by unclean spirits, their speedy healing from Thee, O God, and their salvation.

Remember, O Lord, every Christian soul in affliction and distress, needing Thy mercy and succor, O God; and the return of the erring.

Remember, O Lord, our fathers and brethren, toiling hard, and ministering unto us, for Thy holy name's sake.

Remember all, O Lord, for good: have mercy on all, O Lord, be reconciled to us all: give peace to the multitudes of Thy people: put away scandals: bring wars to an end: make the uprising of heresies to cease: grant Thy peace and Thy love to us, O God our Savior, the hope of all the ends of the earth.

Remember, O Lord, favorable weather, peaceful showers, beneficent dews, abundance of fruits, and to crown the year with Thy goodness; for the eyes of all wait on Thee, and

Thou gives their food in due season: thou opens Thy hand, and fills every living thing with gladness.

Remember, O Lord, those who bear fruit, and labor honorably in the holy of Thy Church; and those who forget not the poor, the widows, the orphans, the strangers, and the needy; and all who have desired us to remember them in our prayers.

Moreover, O Lord, be pleased to remember those who have brought these offerings this day to Thy holy altar, and for what each one has brought them or with what mind, and those persons who have just now been mentioned to Thee.

Remember, O Lord, according to the multitude of Thy mercy and compassion, me also, Thy humble and unprofitable servant; and the deacons who surround Thy holy altar, and graciously give them a blameless life, keep their ministry undefiled, and purchase for them a good degree, that we may find mercy and grace, with all the saints that have been well pleasing to Thee since the world began, to generation and generation—grandsires, sires, patriarchs, prophets, apostles, martyrs, confessors, teachers, saints, and every just spirit made perfect in the faith of Thy Christ.

XXXV. Hail, Mary, highly favored: the Lord is with Thee; blessed art thou among women, and blessed the fruit of thy womb, for thou didst bear the Savior of our souls.

The Deacons.

XXXVI. Remember us, O Lord God.

The Priest, bowing, says:—

Remember, O Lord God, the spirits and all flesh, of whom we have made mention, and of whom we have not made mention, who are of the true faith, from righteous Abel unto this day: unto them do Thou give rest there in the land of the living, in Thy kingdom, in the joy of paradise, in the bosom of Abraham, and of Isaac, and of Jacob, our holy fathers; whence pain, and grief, and lamentation have fled: there the light of Thy countenance looks upon them, and enlightens them forever.

Make the end of our lives Christian, acceptable, blameless, and peaceful, O Lord, gathering us together, O Lord, under the feet of Thine elect, when Thou wilt, and as Thou wilt; only without shame and transgressions, through Thy only-begotten Son, our Lord and God and Savior Jesus Christ: for He is the only sinless one who hath appeared on the earth.

The Deacon.

And *let us pray:*—

For the peace and establishing of the whole world, and of the holy churches of God, and for the purposes for which each one made his offering, or according to the desire he has: and for the people standing round, and for all men, and all women:

The People.

And for all men and all women. (*Amen.*)

The Priest says aloud:—

Wherefore, both to them and to us, do Thou in Thy goodness and love:

The People.

Forgive, remit, pardon, O God, our transgressions, voluntary and involuntary: in deed and in word: in knowledge and in ignorance: by night and by day: in thought and intent: in

Thy goodness and love, forgive us them all.

The Priest.

Through the grace and compassion and love of Thy only-begotten Son, with whom Thou art blessed and glorified, together with the all-holy, and good, and quickening Spirit, now and ever, and to all eternity.

The People.

Amen.

The Priest.

XXXVII. Peace be to all:

The People.

And to thy spirit.

The Deacon.

Again, and continually, in peace let us pray to the Lord.

For the gifts to the Lord God presented and sanctified, precious, heavenly, unspeakable, pure, glorious, dread, awful, divine;

Let us pray.

That the Lord our God, having graciously received them to His altar that is holy and above the heavens, rational and spiritual, for the odor of a sweet spiritual savor, may send down in answer upon us the divine grace and the gift of the all-holy Spirit;

Let us pray.

Having prayed for the unity of the faith, and the communion of His all-holy and adorable Spirit;

Let us commend ourselves and one another, and our whole life, to Christ our God:

The People.

Amen.

The Priest prays.

XXXVIII. God and Father of our Lord and God and Savior Jesus Christ, the glorious Lord, the blessed essence, the bounteous goodness, the God and Sovereign of all, who art blessed to all eternity, who sits upon the cherubim, and art glorified by the seraphim, before whom stand thousand thousands and ten thousand times ten thousand hosts of angels and archangels: Thou hast accepted the gifts, offerings, and fruits brought unto Thee as an odor of a sweet spiritual smell, and hast been pleased to sanctify them, and make them perfect, O good One, by the grace of Thy Christ, and by the presence of Thy all-holy Spirit.

Sanctify also, O Lord, our souls, and bodies, and spirits, and touch our understandings, and search our consciences, and cast out from us every evil imagination, every impure feeling, every base desire, every unbecoming thought, all envy, and vanity, and hypocrisy, all lying, all deceit, every worldly affection, all covetousness, all vainglory, all indifference, all vice, all passion, all anger, all malice, all blasphemy, every motion of the flesh and spirit that is not in accordance with Thy holy will:

(Aloud.)

And count us worthy, O loving Lord, with boldness, without condemnation, in a pure heart, with a contrite spirit, with unashamed face, with sanctified lips, to dare to call upon

Thee, the holy God, Father in heaven, and to say,
The People.

Our Father, which art in heaven: hollowed be Thy name; *and so on to the doxology.*

The Priest, bowing, says (the Embolism):—

And lead us not into temptation, Lord, Lord of Hosts, who knows our frailty, but deliver us from the evil one and his works, and from all his malice and craftiness, for the sake of Thy holy name, which has been placed upon our humility:

(Aloud.)

For Thine is the kingdom, the power, and the glory, Father, Son, and Holy Spirit, now and forever.
The People.
Amen.
The Priest.
XXXIX. Peace be to all.
The People.
And to thy spirit.
The Deacon.
Let us bow our heads to the Lord.
The People.
To Thee, O Lord.
The Priest prays, speaking thus:—

To Thee, O Lord, we Thy servants have bowed our heads before Thy holy altar, waiting for the rich mercies that are from Thee.

Send forth upon us, O Lord, Thy plenteous grace and Thy blessing; and sanctify our souls, bodies, and spirits, that we may become worthy communicants and partakers of Thy holy mysteries, to the forgiveness of sins and life everlasting:

(Aloud.)

For adorable and glorified art Thou, our God, and Thy only-begotten Son, and Thy all Holy Spirit, now and ever.

The People.

Amen.

The Priest says aloud:—

And the grace and the mercies of the holy and consubstantial, and uncreated, and adorable Trinity, shall be with us all.

The People.

And with thy spirit.

The Deacon.

In the fear of God, let us attend.

The Priest says secretly:—

O holy Lord, that abides in holy places, sanctify us by the word of Thy grace, and by the visitation of Thy all-holy Spirit: for Thou, O Lord, hast said, Ye will be holy, for I am holy. O Lord our God, incomprehensible Word of God, one in substance with the Father and the Holy Spirit, co-eternal and indivisible, accept the pure hymn, in Thy holy and bloodless sacrifices; with the cherubim, and seraphim, and from me, a sinful man, crying and saying:—

He takes up the gifts and says aloud:—

XL. The holy things unto holy.

The People.

One *only is* holy, one Lord Jesus Christ, to the glory of God the Father, to whom be glory to all eternity.

The Deacon.

XLI. For the remission of our sins, and the propitiation of our souls, and for every soul in tribulation and distress, needing the mercy and succor of God, and for the return of the erring, the healing of the sick, the deliverance of the captives, the rest of our fathers and brethren who have fallen asleep aforetime;

Let us all say fervently, Lord, have mercy:

The People (twelve times).

Lord, have mercy.

Then the Priest breaks the bread, and holds the half in his right hand, and the half in his left, and dips that in his right hand in the chalice, saying:—

The union of the all-holy body and precious blood of our Lord and God and Savior, Jesus Christ.

Then he makes the sign of the cross on that in his left hand: then with that which has been signed the other half: then forthwith he begins to divide, and before all to give to each chalice a single piece, saying:—

It has been made one, and sanctified, and perfected, in the name of the Father, and of the Son, and of the Holy Spirit, now and ever.

And when he makes the sign of the cross on the bread, he says:—

Behold the Lamb of God, the Son of the Father, that taketh away the sin of the world, sacrificed for the life and salvation of the world.

And when he gives a single piece to each chalice he says:—

A holy portion of Christ, full of grace and truth, of the Father, and of the Holy Spirit, to whom be the glory and the power to all eternity.

Then he begins to divide, and to say:—

XLII. The Lord is my Shepherd, I shall not want. In green pastures, *and so on.*

Then,

I will bless the Lord at all times, *and so on.*

Then,

I will extol Thee, my God, O King, *and so on.*

Then,

O praise the Lord, all ye nations, *and so on.*

The Deacon.

Sir, pronounce the blessing.

The Priest.

The Lord will bless us, and keep us without condemnation for the communion of His pure gifts, now and always, and forever.

And when they have filled, the Deacon says:—

Sir, pronounce the blessing.

The Priest says:—

The Lord will bless us, and make us worthy with the pure touching of our fingers to take the live coal, and place it upon the mouths of the faithful for the purification and renewal of their souls and bodies, now and always.

Then,

O taste and see that the Lord is good; who is parted and not divided; distributed to the faithful and not expended; for the remission of sins, and the life everlasting; now and always, and forever.

The Deacon.

In the peace of Christ, let us sing:

The Singers.

O taste and see that the Lord is good.

The Priest says the prayer before the communion.

O Lord our God, the heavenly bread, the life of the universe, I have sinned against Heaven, and before Thee, and am not worthy to partake of Thy pure mysteries; but as a merciful God, make me worthy by Thy grace, without condemnation to partake of Thy holy body and precious blood, for the remission of sins, and life everlasting.

XLIII. Then he distributes to the clergy; and when the deacons take the disks and the chalices for distribution to the people, the Deacon, who takes the first disk, says:—

Sir, pronounce the blessing.

The Priest replies:—

Glory to God who has sanctified and is sanctifying us all.

The Deacon says:—

Be Thou exalted, O God, over the heavens, and Thy glory over all the earth, and Thy kingdom endures to all eternity.

And when the Deacon is about to put it on the side-table the Priest says:—

Blessed be the name of the Lord our God forever.

The Deacon.

In the fear of God, and in faith and love, draw nigh.

The People.

Blessed is He that cometh in the name of the Lord.

And again, when he sets down the disk upon the side-table, he says:—

Sir, pronounce the blessing.

The Priest.

Save Thy people, O God, and bless Thine inheritance.

The Priest again.

Glory to our God, who has sanctified us all.

And when he has put the chalice back on the holy table, the Priest says:—

Blessed be the name of the Lord to all eternity.

The Deacons and the People say:—

Fill our mouths with Thy praise, O Lord, and fill our lips with joy, that we may sing of Thy glory, of Thy greatness all the day.

And again:—

We render thanks to Thee, Christ our God, that Thou hast made us worthy to partake of Thy body and blood, for the remission of sins, and for life everlasting. Do Thou, in Thy goodness and love, keep us, we pray Thee, without condemnation.

The prayer of incense at the last entrance.

XLIV. We render thanks to Thee, the Savior and God of all, for all the good things Thou hast given us, and for the participation of Thy holy and pure mysteries, and we offer to Thee this incense, praying: Keep us under the shadow of Thy wings, and count us worthy till our last breath to partake of Thy holy rites for the sanctification of our souls and bodies, for the inheritance of the kingdom of heaven: for Thou, O God, art our sanctification, and we send up praise and thanksgiving to Thee, Father, Son, and Holy Spirit.

The Deacon begins in the entrance.

Glory to Thee, glory to Thee, glory to Thee, O Christ the King, only-begotten Word of the Father, that Thou hast counted us, Thy sinful and unworthy servants, worthy to enjoy thy pure mysteries for the remission of sins, and for life everlasting: glory to Thee.

And when he has made the entrance, the Deacon begins to speak thus:—

XLV. Again and again, and at all times, in peace, let us beseech the Lord.

That the participation of His Holy rites may be to us for the turning away from every wicked thing, for our support on the journey to life everlasting, for the communion and gift of the Holy Spirit;

Let us pray.

The Priest prays.

Commemorating our all-holy, pure, most glorious, blessed Lady, the God-Mother and Ever-Virgin Mary, and all the saints that have been well-pleasing to Thee since the world began, let us devote ourselves, and one another, and our whole life, to Christ our God:

The People.

To Thee, O Lord.

The Priest.

XLVI. O God, who through Thy great and unspeakable love didst condescend to the weakness of Thy servants, and hast counted us worthy to partake of this heavenly table, condemn not us sinners for the participation of Thy pure mysteries; but keep us, O good One, in the sanctification of Thy Holy Spirit, that being made holy, we may find part and inheritance with all Thy saints that have been well-pleasing to Thee since the world began, in the light of Thy countenance, through the mercy of Thy only-begotten Son, our Lord and God and

Savior Jesus Christ, with whom Thou art blessed, together with Thy all-holy, and good, and quickening Spirit: for blessed and glorified is Thy all-precious and glorious name, Father, Son, and Holy Spirit, now and ever, and to all eternity.

> The People.
> Amen.
> The Priest.
> Peace be to all.
> The People.
> And to thy spirit.
> The Deacon.
> XLVII. Let us bow our heads to the Lord.
> The Priest.

O God, great and marvelous, look upon Thy servants, for we have bowed our heads to Thee. Stretch forth Thy hand, strong and full of blessings, and bless Thy people. Keep Thine inheritance, that always and at all times we may glorify Thee, our only living and true God, the holy and consubstantial Trinity, Father, Son, and Holy Ghost, now and ever, and to all eternity.

> (Aloud.)

For unto Thee is becoming and is due praise from us all, and honor, and adoration, and thanksgiving, Father, Son, and Holy Spirit, now and ever.

> The Deacon.
> XLVIII. In the peace of Christ let us sing:
> And again he says:—
> In the peace of Christ let us go on:
> The People.

In the name of the Lord. Sir, pronounce the blessing.

Dismission prayer, spoken by the Deacon.

Going on from glory to glory, we praise Thee, the Savior of our souls. Glory to Father, and Son, and Holy Spirit now and ever, and to all eternity. We praise Thee, the Savior of our souls.

The Priest says a prayer from the altar to the sacristy.

XLIX. Going on from strength to strength, and having fulfilled all the divine service in Thy temple, even now we beseech Thee, O Lord our God, make us worthy of perfect lovingkindness; make straight our path: root us in Thy fear, and make us worthy of the heavenly kingdom, in Christ Jesus our Lord, with whom Thou art blessed, together with Thy all-holy, and good, and quickening Spirit, now and always, and forever.

The Deacon.

L. Again and again, and at all times, in peace let us beseech the Lord.

Prayer said in the sacristy after the dismissal.

Thou hast given unto us, O Lord, sanctification in the communion of the all-holy body and precious blood of Thy only-begotten Son, our Lord Jesus Christ; give unto us also the grace of Thy good Spirit, and keep us blameless in the faith, lead us unto perfect adoption and redemption, and to the coming joys of eternity; for Thou art our sanctification and light, O God, and Thy only-begotten Son, and Thy all-holy Spirit, now and ever, and to all eternity. Amen.

The Deacon.

In the peace of Christ let us keep watch.

The Priest.

Blessed is God, who blesses and sanctifies through the communion of the holy, and quickening, and pure mysteries, now and ever, and to all eternity. Amen.

Then the prayer of propitiation.

O Lord Jesus Christ, Son of the living God, Lamb and Shepherd, who takes away the sin of the world, who didst freely forgive their debt to the two debtors, and gives remission of her sins to the woman that was a sinner, who gives healing to the paralytic, with the remission of his sins; forgive, remit, pardon, O God, our offences, voluntary and involuntary, in knowledge and in ignorance, by transgression and by disobedience, which Thy all-holy Spirit knows better than Thy servants do:

And if men, carnal and dwelling in this world, have in aught erred from Thy commandments, either moved by the devil, whether in word or in deed, or if they have come under a curse, or by reason of some special vow, I entreat and beseech Thy unspeakable lovingkindness, that they may be set free from their word, and released from the oath and the special vow, according to Thy goodness.

Verily, O Sovereign Lord, hear my supplication on behalf of Thy servants, and do Thou pass by all their errors, remembering them no more; forgive them every transgression, voluntary and involuntary; deliver them from everlasting punishment: for Thou art He that hast commanded us, saying, Whatsoever things ye bind upon earth, shall be bound in heaven; and whatsoever things ye loose upon earth, shall be loosed in heaven: for, thou art our God, a God able to pity, and to save and to forgive sins; and glory is due unto Thee, with the eternal Father, and the quickening Spirit, now and ever, and to all eternity. Amen.

The Divine Liturgy of the Holy Apostle and Evangelist Mark, The Disciple of the Holy Peter.

The Priest.

I. Peace be to all.

The People.

And to thy spirit.

The Deacon.

Pray.

The People.

Lord, have mercy; Lord, have mercy; Lord, have mercy.

The Priest prays secretly:

We give Thee thanks, yea, more than thanks, O Lord our God, the Father of our Lord and God and Savior Jesus Christ, for all Thy goodness at all times and in all places, because Thou hast shielded, rescued, helped, and guided us all the days of our lives, and brought us unto this hour, permitting us again to stand before Thee in Thy holy place, that we may implore forgiveness of our sins and propitiation to all Thy people. We pray and beseech Thee, merciful God, to grant in Thy goodness that we may spend this holy day and all the time of our lives without sin, in fullness of joy, health, safety, holiness, and reverence of Thee. But all envy, all fear, all temptation, all the influence of Satan, all the snares of wicked men, do Thou, O Lord, drive away from us, and from Thy Holy Catholic and Apostolic Church. Bestow upon us, O Lord, what is good and meet. Whatever sin we commit in thought, word, or deed, do Thou in Thy goodness and mercy be pleased to pardon. Leave us not, O Lord, while we hope in Thee; nor lead us into temptation, but deliver us from the evil one and from his works, through the grace, mercy, and love of Thine only-begotten Son.

(In a loud voice.)

Through whom and with whom be glory and power to Thee, in Thy most holy, good, and life-giving Spirit, now, henceforth, and for evermore.

The People.
Amen.
The Priest.
II. Peace be to all.
The People.
And to thy spirit.
The Deacon.
Pray for the king.
The People.

Lord, have mercy; Lord, have mercy; Lord, have mercy.

The Priest prays.

O God, Sovereign Lord, the Father of our Lord and God and Savior Jesus Christ, we pray and beseech Thee to grant that our king may enjoy peace, and be just and brave. Subdue under him, O God, all his adversaries and enemies. Gird on thy shield and armor, and rise to his aid. Give him the victory, O God, that his heart may be set on peace and the praise of Thy holy name, that we too in his peaceful reign may spend a calm and tranquil life in all reverence and godly fear, through the grace, mercy, and love of Thine only-begotten Son:

(In a loud voice.)

Through whom and with whom be glory and power to Thee, with Thy most holy, good, and life-giving Spirit, now, henceforth, and for evermore.

The People.
Amen.
The Priest.
III. Peace be to all.
The People.
And to thy spirit.
The Deacon.
Pray for the *papas* and the bishop.
The People.

Lord, have mercy; Lord, have mercy; Lord, have mercy.
The Priest.
O Sovereign and Almighty God, the Father of our Lord, God, and Savior Jesus Christ, we pray and beseech Thee to defend in Thy good mercy our most holy and blessed high priest our Father *in God* Δ, and our most reverend Bishop Δ. Preserve them for us through many years in peace, while they according to Thy holy and blessed will fulfil the sacred priesthood committed to their care, and dispense aright the word of truth; with all the orthodox bishops, elders, deacons, sub-deacons, readers, singers, and laity, with the entire body of the Holy and only Catholic Church. Graciously bestow upon them peace, health, and salvation. The prayers they offer up for us, and we for them, do Thou, O Lord, receive at Thy holy, heavenly, and reasonable altar. But all the enemies of Thy Holy Church put Thou speedily under their feet, through the grace, mercy, and love of Thine only-begotten Son:
(Aloud.)

Through whom and with whom be glory and power to Thee, with Thy all-holy, good, and life-giving Spirit, now, henceforth, and for evermore.

The People.
Amen.
The Priest.
IV. Peace be to all.
The People.
And to thy spirit.
The Deacon.
Stand and pray.
The People.
Lord have mercy (*thrice*).

The Priest offers up the prayer of entrance, and for incense.

The Priest.

O Sovereign Lord our God, who hast chosen the lamp of the twelve apostles with its twelve lights, and hast sent them forth to proclaim throughout the whole world and teach the Gospel of Thy kingdom, and to heal sickness and every weakness among the people, and hast breathed upon their faces and said unto them, Receive the Holy Spirit the Comforter: whosesoever sins ye remit, they are remitted unto them; and whosesoever sins ye retain, they are retained: Breathe also Thy Holy Spirit upon us Thy servants, who, standing around, are about to enter on Thy holy service, upon the bishops, elders, deacons, readers, singers, and laity, with the entire body of the Holy Catholic and Apostolic Church.

From the curse and execration, from condemnation, imprisonment, and banishment, and from the portion of the adversary;

O Lord, deliver us.

Purify our lives and cleanse our hearts from all pollution and from all wickedness, that with pure heart and conscience we may offer to Thee this incense for a sweet-smelling savor, and for the remission of our sins and the sins of all Thy people, through the grace, mercy, and love of Thine only-begotten Son:

(Aloud.)

Through whom and with whom be the glory and the power to Thee, with Thy all-holy, good, and life-giving Spirit, now, henceforth, and for evermore.

The People.

Amen.

The Deacon.

V. Stand.

They sing:—

Only-begotten Son and Word, etc.

The Gospel is carried in, and the Deacon says:—

Let us pray.

The Priest.

Peace be to all.

The People.

And to thy spirit.

The Deacon.

Let us pray.

The People.

Lord, have mercy.

The Priest says the prayer of the Trisagion.

O Sovereign Lord Christ Jesus, the co-eternal Word of the eternal Father, who was made in all things like as we are, but without sin, for the salvation of our race; who hast sent forth Thy holy disciples and apostles to proclaim and teach the Gospel of Thy kingdom, and to heal all disease, all sickness among Thy people, be pleased now, O Lord, to send forth Thy light and Thy truth. Enlighten the eyes of our minds, that we may understand Thy divine oracles. Fit us to become hearers, and not only hearers, but doers of Thy word, that we, becoming fruitful, and yielding good fruit from thirty to an hundred fold, may be deemed worthy of the kingdom of heaven.

(Aloud.)

Let Thy mercy speedily overtake us, O Lord. For Thou art the bringer of good tidings, the Savior and Guardian of our souls and bodies; and we offer glory, thanks, and the Trisagion to Thee, the Father, Son, and Holy Ghost, now, henceforth, and for evermore.

The People.

Amen. Holy God, holy mighty, holy immortal. Holy, holy, holy, etc.

VI. After the Trisagion the Priest makes the sign of the cross over the people, and says:—

Peace be to all.

The People.

And to thy spirit.

Then follow the Let us attend; The Apostle and Prologue of the Hallelujah. The

Deacons, after a prescribed form, say:—

Lord, bless us.

The Priest says:—

May the Lord in His mercy bless and help us, now, henceforth, and for evermore.

The Priest, before the Gospel is read, offers incense, and says:—

Accept at Thy holy, heavenly, and reasonable altar, O Lord, the incense we offer in presence of Thy sacred glory. Send down upon us in return the grace of

Thy Holy Spirit, for Thou art blessed, and let Thy glory encircle us.

VII. The Deacon, when he is about to read the Gospel, says:—

Lord, bless us.

The Priest.

May the Lord, who is the blessed God, bless and strengthen us, and make us hearers of His holy Gospel, now, henceforth, and for evermore. Amen.

The Deacon.
Stand and let us hear the holy Gospel.
The Priest.
Peace be to all.
The People.
And to thy spirit.

VIII. The Deacon reads the Gospel, and the Priest says the prayer of the Collect. Look down in mercy and compassion, O Lord, and heal the sick among Thy people. May all our brethren who have gone or who are about to go abroad, safely reach their destination in due season.

Send down the gracious rain upon the thirsty lands, and make the rivers flow in full stream, according to Thy grace.

The fruits of the land do Thou, O Lord, fill with seed and make ripe for the harvest.

In peace, courage, justice, and tranquility preserve the kingdom of Thy servant, whom

Thou hast deemed worthy to reign over this land.

From evil days, from famine and pestilence, from the assault of barbarians, defend, O

Lord, this Christ-loving city, lowly and worthy of Thy compassion, as Thou didst spare

Nineveh of old.

For Thou art full of mercy and compassion, and remembers not the iniquities of men against them.

Thou hast said through Thy prophet Isaiah,—I will defend this city, to save it for mine own sake, and for my servant David's sake.

Wherefore we pray and beseech Thee to defend in Thy good mercy this city, for the sake of the martyr and evangelist Mark, who has shown us the way of salvation through the grace, mercy, and love of Thine only-begotten Son.

(Aloud.)

Through whom and with whom be glory and power to Thee, with Thy all-holy, good, and life-giving Spirit.

The Deacon.

IX. Begin.

Then they say the verse. The Deacon says—The three.

The Priest.

O Sovereign and Almighty God, the Father of our Lord Jesus Christ, we pray and beseech Thee to fill our hearts with the peace of heaven, and to bestow moreover the peace of this life. Preserve for us through many years our most holy and blessed *Papas* Δ, and our most pious Bishop Δ, while they, according to Thy holy and blessed will, peacefully fulfil the holy priesthood committed to their care, and dispense aright the word of truth, with all the orthodox bishops, elders, deacons, sub-deacons, readers, singers, with the entire body of the holy Catholic and Apostolic Church. Bless our meetings, O Lord. Grant that we may hold them without let or hindrance, according to Thy holy will. Be pleased to give to us, and Thy servants after us forever, houses of praise and prayer. Rise, O Lord, and let Thine enemies be scattered. Let all who hate Thy holy name be put to flight. Bless Thy faithful and orthodox people. Multiply them by thousands and tens of thousands. Let no deadly sin prevail against them, or against Thy holy people, through the grace, mercy, and love of Thine only-begotten Son.

(Aloud.)

Through whom and with whom be glory and power to Thee, with Thy all-holy, good, and life-giving Spirit.

The People.
Amen.
The Priest.
Peace be to all.
The People.
And to thy spirit.
The Deacon.
Take care that none of the catechumens—

II.

Then they sing the Cherubic hymn.

X. The Priest offers incense at the entrance, and prays:—

O Lord our God, who lacks nothing, accept this incense offered by an unworthy hand, and deem us all worthy of Thy blessing, for Thou art our sanctification, and we ascribe glory to Thee.

The holy things are carried to the altar, and the Priest prays thus:—

O holy, highest, awe-inspiring God, who dwells among the saints, sanctify us, and deem us worthy of Thy reverend priesthood. Bring us to Thy precious altar with a good conscience, and cleanse our hearts from all pollution. Drive away from us all unholy thoughts, and sanctify our souls and minds. Grant that, with reverence of Thee, we may perform the service of our holy fathers, and propitiate Thy presence through all time; for Thou art He who blesses and sanctifies all things, and to Thee we ascribe glory and thanks.

The Deacon.

XI. Salute one another.

The Priest says the prayer of salutation.

O Sovereign and Almighty Lord, look down from heaven on Thy Church, on all Thy people, and on all Thy flock. Save us all, Thy unworthy servants, the sheep of Thy fold. Give us Thy peace, Thy help, and Thy love, and send to us the gift of Thy Holy Spirit, that with a pure heart and a good conscience we may salute one another with an holy kiss, without hypocrisy, and with no hostile purpose, but guileless and pure in one spirit, in the bond of peace and love, one body and one spirit, in one faith, even as we have been called in one hope of our calling, that we may all meet in the divine and boundless love, in Christ Jesus our Lord, with whom Thou art blessed.

Then the Priest offers the incense, and says:—

The incense is offered to Thy name. Let it ascend, we implore Thee, from the hands of

Thy poor and sinful servants to Thy heavenly altar for a sweet-smelling savor, and the propitiation of all Thy people. For all glory, honor, adoration, and thanks are due unto Thee, the Father, Son, and Holy Ghost, now, henceforth, and for evermore. Amen.

After the Salutation, the Deacon in a loud voice says:—

XII. Stand and make the offering duly.

The Priest, making the sign of the cross over the disks and chalices, says in a loud voice
(The Nicene Creed):—
I believe in one God, etc.
The Deacon.
Stand for prayer.
The Priest.
Peace be to all.
The Deacon.
Pray for those who present the offering.
The Priest says the prayer of the Oblation.

O Sovereign Lord, Christ Jesus the Word, who art equal in power with the Father and the Holy Spirit, the great high priest; the bread that came down from heaven, and saved our souls from ruin; who gives Thyself, a spotless Lamb, for the life of the world....

We pray and beseech Thee, O Lord, in Thy mercy, to let Thy presence rest upon this bread and these chalices on the all-holy table, while angels, archangels, and Thy holy priests stand round and minister for Thy glory and the renewing of our souls, through the grace, mercy, and love of Thine only-begotten Son, through whom and with whom be glory and power to Thee.

And when the People say,
And from the Holy Spirit was He made flesh;
The Priest makes the sign of the cross, and says:—
And was crucified for us.
The Priest makes the sign of the cross again, and says:—
And to the Holy Spirit.

III.

XIII. In like manner also, as after the Creed, he makes the sign of the cross upon the People, and says aloud:—

The Lord be with all.
The People.
And with thy spirit.
The Priest.
Let us lift up our hearts.
The People.
We lift them up to the Lord.
The Priest.
Let us give thanks to the Lord.
The People.
It is meet and right.
The Priest begins the Anaphoral prayer.

O Lord God, Sovereign and Almighty Father, truly it is meet and right, holy and becoming, and good for our souls, to praise, bless, and thank Thee; to make open confession to Thee by day and night with voice, lips, and heart without ceasing;

To Thee who hast made the heaven, and all that is therein; the earth, and all that is therein; The sea, fountains, rivers, lakes, and all that is therein;

To Thee who, after Thine own image and likeness, hast made man, upon whom Thou didst also bestow the joys of Paradise;

And when he trespassed against Thee, Thou didst neither neglect nor forsake him, good Lord,

But didst recall him by Thy law, instruct him by Thy prophets, restore and renew him by this awful, life-giving, and heavenly mystery.

And all this Thou hast done by Thy Wisdom and the Light of truth, Thine only-begotten Son, our Lord, God, and Savior Jesus Christ, Through whom, thanking Thee with Him and the Holy Spirit,

We offer this reasonable and bloodless sacrifice, which all nations, from the rising to the setting of the sun, from the north and the south, present to Thee, O Lord; for great is Thy name among all peoples, and in all places are incense, sacrifice, and oblation offered to Thy holy name.

XIV. We pray and beseech Thee, *O lover of men, O good* Lord, remember in Thy good mercy the Holy and only Catholic and Apostolic Church throughout the whole world, and all Thy people, and all the sheep of this fold. Vouchsafe to the hearts of all of us the peace of heaven, but grant us also the peace of this life.

Guide and direct in all peace the king, army, magistrates, councils, peoples, and neighborhoods, and all our outgoings and incomings.

O King of Peace, grant us Thy peace in unity and love. May we be Thine, O Lord; for we know no other God but Thee, and name no other name but Thine. Give life unto the souls of all of us, and let no deadly sin prevail against us, or against all Thy people.

Look down in mercy and compassion, O Lord, and heal the sick among Thy people.

Deliver them and us, O Lord, from sickness and disease, and drive away the spirit of weakness.

Raise up those who have been long afflicted, and heal those who are vexed with unclean spirits.

Have mercy on all who are in prison, or in mines, or on trial, or condemned, or in exile, or crushed by cruel bondage or tribute. Deliver them, O Lord, for Thou art our God, who sets the captives free; who raises up the downtrodden; who gives hope to the hopeless, and help to the helpless; who lifts up the fallen; who gives refuge to the shipwrecked, and vengeance to the oppressed.

Pity, relieve, and restore every Christian soul that is afflicted or wandering.

But do Thou, O Lord, the physician of our souls and bodies, the guardian of all flesh, look down, and by Thy saving power heal all the diseases of soul and body.

Guide and prosper our brethren who have gone or who are about to go abroad.

Whether they travel by land, or river, or lake, by public road, or in whatever way journeying, bring them everywhere to a safe and tranquil haven. Be pleased to be with them by land and sea, and restore them in health and joy to joyful and healthful homes.

Ever defend, O Lord, our journey through this life from trouble and storm.

Send down rich and copious showers on the dry and thirsty lands.

Gladden and revive the face of the earth, that it may spring forth and rejoice in the raindrops.

Make the waters of the river flow in full stream.

Gladden and revive the face of the earth with the swelling waters.

Fill all the channels of the streams, and multiply the fruits of the earth.

Bless, O Lord, the fruits of the earth, and keep them safe and unharmed. Fill them with seed, and make them ripe for the harvest.

Bless even now, O Lord, Thy yearly crown of blessing for the sake of the poor of Thy people, the widow, the orphan, and the stranger, and for the sake of all of us who have our hope in Thee and call upon Thy holy name; for the eyes of all are upon Thee, and Thou gives them bread in due season.

O Thou who gives food to all flesh, fill our hearts with joy and gladness, that at all times, having all sufficiency, we may abound to every good work in Christ Jesus our Lord.

O King of kings and Lord of lords, defend the kingdom of Thy servant, our orthodox and Christ-loving sovereign, whom Thou hast deemed worthy to reign over this land in peace, courage, and justice.

Subdue under him, O Lord, every enemy and adversary, whether at home or abroad. Gird on Thy shield and armor, and rise to his aid. Draw Thy sword, and help him to fight against them that persecute him. Shield him in the day of battle, and grant that the fruit of his loins may sit upon his throne.

Be kind to him, O Lord, for the sake of Thy Holy and Apostolic Church, and all Thy Christ-loving people, that we too in his peaceful reign may live a calm and tranquil life, in all reverence and godliness.

O Lord our God, give peace to the souls of our fathers and brethren who have fallen asleep in Jesus, remembering our forefathers of old, our fathers, patriarchs, prophets, apostles, martyrs, confessors, bishops, and the souls of all the holy and just men who have died in the Lord.

Especially remember those whose memory we this day *celebrate*, and our holy father Mark, the apostle and evangelist, who has shown us the way of salvation.

The Deacon.

Lord, bless us.

The Priest.

The Lord will bless thee in His grace, now, henceforth, and for evermore.

The Deacon reads the record of the dead.

The Priest bows and prays.

XV. Give peace, O Sovereign Lord our God, to the souls of all who dwell in the tabernacles of Thy saints. Graciously bestow upon them in Thy kingdom Thy promised blessing, which eye hath not seen, and ear hath not heard, nor has it entered into the heart of man what Thou, O God, hast prepared for those who love Thy holy name. Give peace to their souls, and deem them worthy of the kingdom of heaven.

Grant that we may end our lives as Christians, acceptable unto Thee and without sin, and be pleased to give us part and lot with all Thy saints.

Accept, O God, by Thy ministering archangels at Thy holy, heavenly, and reasonable altar in the spacious heavens, the thank-offerings of those who offer sacrifice and oblation, and of those who desire to offer much or little, in secret or openly, but have it not to give.

Accept the thank-offerings of those who have presented them this day, as Thou didst accept the gifts of Thy righteous Abel:

The Priest offers incense, and says:—

As Thou didst accept the sacrifice of our father Abraham, the incense of Zacharias, the alms of Cornelius, and the widow's two mites, accept also the thank-offerings of these, and give them for the things of time the things of eternity, and for the things of earth the things of heaven. Defend, O Lord, our most holy and blessed *Papas* Δ, whom Thou hast foreordained to rule over Thy Holy

Catholic and Apostolic Church, and our most pious Bishop

Δ, that they through many years of peace may, according to Thy holy and blessed will, fulfil the sacred priesthood committed to their care, and dispense aright the word of truth.

Remember the orthodox bishops everywhere, the elders, deacons, sub-deacons, readers, singers, monks, virgins, widows, and laity.

Remember, O Lord, the holy city of our God, Jesus Christ; and the imperial city; and this city of ours, and all cities and all lands, and the peace and safety of those who dwell therein in the orthodox faith of Christ.

Be mindful, O Lord, of the return of the backsliding, and of every Christian soul that is afflicted and oppressed, and in need of Thy divine mercy and help.

Be mindful, O Lord, of our brethren in captivity. Grant that they may find mercy and compassion with those who have led them captive.

Be mindful also of us, O Lord, Thy sinful and unworthy servants, and blot out our sins in Thy goodness and mercy.

Be mindful also of me, Thy lowly, sinful, and unworthy servant, and in Thy mercy blot out my sins. Be with us, O Lord, who minister unto Thy holy name.

Bless our meetings, O Lord.

Utterly uproot idolatry from the world.

Crush under our feet Satan, and all his wicked influence.

Humble now, as at all times, the enemies of Thy Church.

Lay bare their pride.

Speedily show them their weakness.

Bring to naught the wicked plots they contrive against us.

Arise, O Lord, and let Thine enemies be scattered, and let all who hate Thy holy name be put to flight.

Do Thou bless a thousand times ten thousand Thy faithful and orthodox people while they do Thy holy will.

The Deacon.

Let those who are seated stand.

The Priest says the following prayer:—

Deliver the captive; rescue the distressed feed the hungry; comfort the faint-hearted, convert the erring; enlighten the darkened; raise the fallen; confirm the wavering; heal the sick; and guide them all, good Lord, into the way of salvation, and into Thy sacred fold.

Deliver us from our iniquities; protect and defend us at all times.

The Deacon.

Turn to the east.

The Priest bows and prays.

For Thou art far above all principality, and power, and might, and dominion, and every name that is named, not only in this world, but in that which is to come. Round Thee stand ten thousand times ten thousand, and thousands of thousands of holy angels and hosts of archangels; and Thy two most honored creatures, the many-eyed cherubim and the six winged seraphim. With twain they cover their faces, and with twain they cover their feet, and with twain they do fly; and they cry one to another forever with the voice of praise, and glorify Thee, O Lord, singing aloud the triumphal and thrice-holy hymn to Thy great glory:—

Holy, holy, holy, Lord God of Sabbath. Heaven and earth are full of Thy glory.

(Aloud.)

Thou dost ever sanctify all men; but with all who glorify Thee, receive also, O Sovereign

Lord, our sanctification, who with them celebrate Thy praise, and say:—

The People.

Holy, holy, holy Lord.

The Priest makes the sign of the cross over the sacred mysteries.

XVI. For truly heaven and earth are full of Thy glory, through the manifestation of our

Lord and God and Savior Jesus Christ. Fill, O God, this sacrifice with Thy blessing, through the inspiration of Thy all-holy Spirit. For the Lord Himself, our God and universal King,

Christ Jesus, reclining at meat the same night on which He delivered Himself up for our sins and died in the flesh for all, took bread in His holy, pure, and immaculate hands, and lifting His eyes to His Father, our God, and the God of all, gave thanks; and when He had blessed, hallowed, and broken the bread, gave it to His holy and blessed disciples and apostles, saying:—

(Aloud.)

Take, eat.

The Deacon.

Pray earnestly.

The Priest (aloud).

For this is my body, which is broken for you, and divided for the remission of sins.

The People.

Amen.

The Priest prays.

After the same manner also, when He had supped, He took the cup of wine mingled with water, and lifting His eyes to Thee, His Father, our God, and the God of all, gave thanks; and when He had blessed and filled it with the Holy Spirit, gave it to His holy and blessed disciples and apostles, saying:—

(Aloud.)

Drink ye all of it.

The Deacon.

Pray earnestly again.

The Priest (aloud).

For this is my blood of the New Testament which is shed for you and for many, and distributed among you for the remission of sins.

The People.

Amen.

The Priest prays thus:—

This do ye in remembrance of me; for as often as ye eat this bread and drink this cup, ye do show forth my death and acknowledge my resurrection and ascension until I come. O Sovereign and Almighty Lord, King of heaven, while we show forth the death of Thine only-begotten Son, our Lord, God, and Savior Jesus Christ, and acknowledge His blessed resurrection from the dead on the third day, we do also openly declare His ascension into heaven, and His sitting on the right hand of Thee, God and Father, and await His second terrible and dreadful coming, in which He will come to judge righteously the quick and the dead, and to render to each man according to his works.

XVII. O Lord our God, we have placed before Thee what is Thine from Thine own mercies. We pray and beseech Thee, O good and merciful God, to send down from Thy holy heaven, from the mansion Thou hast prepared, and from Thine infinite bosom, the Paraclete Himself, holy, powerful, and life-giving, the Spirit of truth, who spoke in the law, the apostles, and prophets; who is everywhere present, and fills all things, freely working sanctification in whom He will with Thy good pleasure; one in His nature; manifold in His working; the fountain of divine blessing; of like substance with Thee, and proceeding from Thee; sitting with Thee on the throne of Thy kingdom, and with Thine only-begotten Son, our Lord and God and Savior Jesus Christ. Send down upon us also and upon this bread and upon these chalices Thy Holy Spirit, that by His all-powerful and divine influence He may sanctify and consecrate them, and make this bread the body.

The People.

Amen.

The Priest (aloud).

And this cup the blood of the new testament, of the very Lord, and God, and Savior, and universal King Christ Jesus.

The Deacon.

Deacons, come down.

The Priest (aloud).

That to all of us who partake thereof they may tend unto faith, sobriety, healing, temperance, sanctification, the renewal of soul, body, and spirit, participation in the blessedness of eternal life and immortality, the glory of Thy most holy name, and the remission of sins, that Thy most holy, precious, and glorious name may be praised and glorified in this as in all things.

The People.

As it was and is.

The Priest.

XVIII. Peace be to all.

The Deacon.

Pray.

The Priest prays in secret.

O God of light, Father of life, Author of grace, Creator of worlds, Founder of knowledge, Giver of wisdom, Treasure of holiness, Teacher of pure prayers, Benefactor of our souls, who gives to the faint-hearted who put their trust in Thee those things into which the angels desire to look: O Sovereign Lord, who hast brought us up from the depths of darkness to light, who hast given us life from death, who hast graciously bestowed upon us freedom from slavery, who hast scattered the darkness of sin within us, through the presence of Thine only-begotten Son, do Thou now also, through the visitation of Thy all-holy Spirit, enlighten the eyes of our understanding, that we may partake without fear of condemnation of this heavenly and immortal food, and sanctify us wholly in soul, body, and spirit, that with Thy holy disciples and apostles we may say this prayer to Thee: Our Father who art in heaven, etc.

(Aloud.)

And grant, O Sovereign Lord, in Thy mercy, that we with freedom of speech, without fear of condemnation, with pure heart and enlightened soul, with face that is not ashamed, and with hollowed lips, may venture to call upon Thee, the holy God who art in heaven, as our Father, and say:—

The People.

Our Father who art in heaven, etc.

The Priest prays:—

Verily, Lord, Lord, lead us not into temptation, but deliver us from evil; for Thy abundant mercy shows that we through our great infirmity are unable to resist it. Grant that we may find a way whereby we may be able to withstand temptation; for Thou hast given us power to tread upon serpents, and scorpions, and all the power of the enemy.

(Aloud.)

For Thine is the kingdom and power.

The People.

Amen.

The Priest.

XIX. Peace be to all.

The Deacon.

Bow your heads to Jesus.

The People.

Thou, Lord.

The Priest prays.

O Sovereign and Almighty Lord, who sits upon the cherubim, and art glorified by the seraphim; who hast made the heaven out of waters, and adorned it with choirs of stars; who hast placed an unbodied host of angels in the highest heavens to sing Thy praise for ever; before Thee have we bowed our souls and bodies in token of our bondage. We beseech Thee to repel the dark assaults of sin from our understanding, and to gladden our minds with the divine radiance of Thy Holy Spirit, that, filled with the knowledge of Thee, we may worthily partake of the mercies set before us, the pure body and precious blood of Thine only-begotten Son, our Lord and God and

Savior Jesus Christ. Pardon all our sins in Thy abundant and unsearchable goodness, through the grace, mercy, and love of Thine only-begotten Son:

(Aloud.)

Through whom and with whom be glory and power to Thee, with the all-holy, good, and life-giving Spirit.

The Priest.

XX. Peace be to all.

The Deacon.

With the fear of God.

The Priest prays.

O holy, highest, awe-inspiring God, who dwells among the saints, sanctify us by the word of Thy grace and by the inspiration of Thy all-holy Spirit; for Thou hast said, O Lord our God, Be ye holy; for I am holy. O Word of God, past finding out, consubstantial and co-eternal with the Father and the Holy Spirit, and sharer of their sovereignty, accept the pure song which cherubim and seraphim, and the unworthy lips of Thy sinful and unworthy servant, sing aloud.

The People.

Lord, have mercy; Lord, have mercy; Lord, have mercy.

The Priest (aloud).

Holy things for the holy.

The People.

One Father Holy, one Son holy, one Spirit holy, in the unity of the Holy Spirit. Amen.

The Deacon.

For salvation and help.

The Priest makes the sign of the cross upon the people, and says in a loud voice:—
The Lord be with all.
The Priest breaks the bread, and says:—
Praise you God.
The Priest divides it among those present, and says:—
The Lord will bless and help you through His great *mercy.*
The Priest says:—
Command.
The Clergy say:—
The Holy Spirit commands and sanctifies.
The Priest.
Lo, they are sanctified and consecrated.

The Clergy.
One Holy Father, etc. (*thrice*).
The Priest says:—
The Lord be with all.
The Clergy.
And with thy spirit.
The Priest says:—
The Lord Himself hath blessed it.
The Priest partakes, and prays.
According to Thy loving-kindness, etc.
Or,
As the hart panted after the water-brooks, etc.
When he gives the bread to the clergy, he says:—
The holy body.
And when he gives the chalice, he says:—
The precious blood of our Lord, and God, and Savior.

IV.

After the service is completed, the Deacon says:—
XXI. Stand for prayer.
The Priest.
Peace be to all.
The Deacon.
Pray.
The Priest says the prayer of thanksgiving.

O Sovereign Lord our God, we thank Thee that we have partaken of Thy holy, pure, immortal, and heavenly mysteries, which Thou hast given for our good, and for the sanctification and salvation of our souls and bodies. We pray and beseech Thee, O Lord, to grant in Thy good mercy, that by partaking of the holy body and precious blood of Thine only begotten Son, we may have faith that is not ashamed, love that is unfeigned, fullness of holiness, power to eschew evil and keep Thy commandments, provision for eternal life, and an acceptable defense before the awful tribunal of Thy Christ:

In a loud voice.

Through whom and with whom be glory and power to Thee, with Thy all-holy, good, and life-giving Spirit.

The Priest then turns to the people, and says:—
XXII. O mightiest King, co-eternal with the Father, who by Thy might hast vanquished hell and trodden death under foot, who hast bound the strong man, and by Thy miraculous power and the enlightening radiance of Thy unspeakable Godhead hast raised Adam

from the tomb, send forth Thy invisible right hand, which is full of blessing, and bless us all.

Pity us, O Lord, and strengthen us by Thy divine power.

Take away from us the sinful and wicked influence of carnal desire.

Let the light shine into our souls, and dispel the surrounding darkness of sin.

Unite us to the all-blessed assembly that is well-pleasing unto Thee; for through Thee and with Thee, all praise, honor, power, adoration, and thanksgiving are due unto the Father and the Holy Spirit, now, henceforth, and for evermore.

The Deacon.

Depart in peace:

The People.

In the name of the Lord.

The Priest (aloud).

XXIII. The love of God the Father; the grace of the Son, our Lord Jesus Christ; the communion and gift of the All-holy Spirit, be with us all, now, henceforth, and for evermore.

The People.

Amen. Blessed be the name of the Lord.

The Priest prays in the sacristy, and says:—

O Lord, Thou hast given us sanctification by partaking of the all-holy body and precious blood of Thine only-begotten Son; give us the grace and gift of the All-holy Spirit. Enable us to lead blameless lives; and guide us unto the perfect redemption, and adoption, and the everlasting joys of the world to come. For Thou art our sanctification, and we ascribe glory unto Thee, the

Father, and the Son, and the All-holy Spirit, now, henceforth, and for evermore.

The People.
Amen.
The Priest.
Peace be to all.
The People.
And to thy spirit.
The Priest dismisses them, and says:—

May God bless, who blesses and sanctifies, who defended and preserves us all through the partaking of His holy mysteries; and who is blessed forever. Amen.

The Liturgy of the Blessed Apostles.

Composed by St. Adæus and St. Maris, Teachers of the Easterns.

I. *First*: Glory to God in the highest, etc. Our Father which art in heaven.
Prayer.
Strengthen, O our Lord and God, our weakness through Thy mercy, that we may administer the holy mystery which has been given for the renovation and salvation of our degraded nature, through the mercies of Thy beloved Son the Lord of all.
On common days.
Adored, glorified, lauded, celebrated, exalted, and blessed in heaven and on earth, be the adorable and glorious name of Thine ever-glorious Trinity, O Lord of all.

On common days they sing the Psalm (xv.), Lord, who shall dwell in Thy tabernacle? *Entire with its canon, of the mystery of the sacraments.*

(Aloud.)

Who shall shout with joy? Etc.

Prayer.

II. Before the resplendent throne of Thy majesty, O Lord, and the exalted and sublime throne of Thy glory, and on the awful seat of the strength of Thy love and the propiatory altar which Thy will hath established, in the region of Thy pasture, with thousands of cherubim praising Thee, and ten thousands of seraphim sanctifying Thee, we draw near, adore, thank, and glorify Thee always, O Lord of all.

On commemorations and Fridays.

Thy name, great and holy, illustrious and blessed, the blessed and incomprehensible name of Thy glorious Trinity, and Thy kindness to our race, we ought at all times to bless, adore, and glorify, O Lord of all.

Responsory at the chancel, as above.

Who commanded, etc.

To the priest, etc.

Prayer.

How breathes in us, O our Lord and God, the sweet fragrance of the sweetness of Thy love; illumined are our souls, through the knowledge of Thy truth: may we be rendered worthy of receiving the manifestation of Thy beloved from Thy holy heavens: there shall we render thanks unto Thee, and, in the meantime, glorify Thee without ceasing in Thy Church, crowned and filled with every aid and blessing, because Thou art Lord and Father,

Creator of all.

III. Prayer of Incense.

We shall repeat the hymn to Thy glorious Trinity, O Father, Son, and Holy Ghost.

On fast-days.

And on account, etc.

At the commemoration of saints.

Thou, O Lord, art truly the raiser up of our bodies: Thou art the good Savior of our souls, and the secure preserver of our life; and we ought to thank Thee continually, to adore and glorify Thee, O Lord of all.

At the lessons.

Holy art Thou, worthy of praise, mighty, immortal, who dwells in the holies, and Thy will rested in them: have regard unto us, O Lord; be merciful unto us, and pity us, as Thou art our helper in all circumstances, O Lord of all.

IV. At the apostle.

Enlighten, O our Lord and God, the movements of our meditations to hear and understand the sweet listening to Thy life-giving and divine commands; and grant unto us through Thy grace and mercy to gather from them the assurance of love, and hope, and salvation suitable to soul and body, and we shall sing to Thee everlasting glory without ceasing and always, O Lord of all.

On fast-days.

To Thee, the wise governor, etc.

V. Descending, he shall salute the Gospel, saying this prayer before the altar.

Thee, the renowned seed of Thy Father, and the image of the person of Thy Father, who was revealed in the body of our humanity, and didst arise to us in the light of Thy annunciation, Thee we thank, adore, etc.

And after the proclamation:—

Thee, O Lord God Almighty, we beseech and entreat, perfect with us Thy grace, and pour out through our hands Thy gift, the pity and compassion of Thy divinity. May they be to us for the propitiation of the offences of Thy people, and for the forgiveness of the sins of the entire flock of Thy pasture, through Thy grace and tender mercies, O good friend of men, O Lord of all.

VI. The Deacons say:—

Bow your heads.

The Priest says this secret prayer in the sanctuary:—

O Lord God Omnipotent, Thine is the Holy Catholic Church, inasmuch as Thou, through the great passion of Thy Christ, didst buy the sheep of Thy pasture; and from the grace of the Holy Spirit, who is indeed of one nature with Thy glorious divinity, are granted the degrees of the true priestly ordination; and through Thy clemency Thou didst vouchsafe, O Lord, to make our weakness spiritual members in the great body of Thy Holy Church, that we might administer spiritual aid to faithful souls. Now, O Lord, perfect Thy grace with us, and pour out Thy gift through our hands: and may Thy tender mercies and the clemency of Thy divinity be upon us, and upon the people whom Thou hast chosen for Thyself.

(Aloud.)

And grant unto us, O Lord, through Thy clemency, that we may all together, and equally every day of our life, please Thy divinity, and be rendered worthy of the aid of Thy grace to offer Thee praise, honor, thanksgiving, and adoration at all times, O Lord.

VII. And the Deacons ascend to the altar, and say:—

He who has not received baptism, etc.

And the Priest begins the responsory of the mysteries, and the Sacristan and Deacon place the disk and the chalice upon the altar. The Priest crosses his hands, and says:—

We offer praise to Thy glorious Trinity at all times and forever.

And proceeds:—

May Christ, who was offered for our salvation, and commanded us to commemorate His death and His resurrection, Himself receive this sacrifice from the hands of our weakness, through His grace and mercies forever. Amen.

And proceeds:—

Laid are the renowned holy and life-giving mysteries upon the altar of the mighty Lord, even until His advent, forever. Amen.

Praise, etc.

Thy memory, etc.

Our Father, etc.

The apostles of the Father, etc.

Upon the holy altar, etc.

They who have slept, etc.

Matthew Mark, Luke, etc.

THE CREED.

VIII. The Priest draws near to celebrate, and thrice bows before the altar, the middle of which he kisses, then the right and the left horn of the altar; and bows to the Gospel side, and says:—

Bless, O Lord, etc.

Pray for me, my fathers, brethren, and masters, that God may grant unto me the capability and power to perform this service to which I have drawn near, and that this oblation may be accepted from the hands of my weakness, for myself, for you, and for the whole body of the Holy Catholic Church, through His grace and mercies forever. Amen.

And they respond:—

May Christ listen to thy prayers, and be pleased with thy sacrifice, receive thy oblation, and honor thy priesthood, and grant unto us, through thy mediation, the pardon of our offences, and the forgiveness of our sins, through His grace and mercies forever.

Presently he bows at the other side, uttering the same words; and they respond in the same manner: then he bows to the altar, and says:—

God, Lord of all, be with us through His grace and mercies forever. Amen.

And bowing towards the Deacon, who is on the left (Epistle side), he says:—

God, the Lord of all, confirm thy words, and secure to thee peace, and accept this oblation from my hands for me, for thee, for the whole body of the Holy Catholic Church, and for the entire world, through His grace and mercies forever.

He kneels at the altar, and says in secret:—

IX. O our Lord and God, look not on the multitude of our sins, and let not Thy dignity be turned away on account of the heinousness of our iniquities; but through Thine unspeakable grace sanctify this sacrifice of Thine, and grant through it power and capability, so that

Thou may forget our many sins, and be merciful when Thou shalt appear at the end of time, in the man whom Thou hast assumed from among us, and we may find before Thee grace and mercy, and be rendered worthy to praise Thee with spiritual assemblies.

He rises, and says this prayer in secret:—

We thank Thee, O our Lord and God, for the abundant riches of Thy grace to us:

And he proceeds:—

Us who were sinful and degraded, on account of the multitude of Thy clemency, Thou hast made worthy to celebrate the holy mysteries of the body and blood of Thy Christ. We beg aid from Thee for the strengthening of our souls, that in perfect love and true faith we may administer Thy gift to us.

Canon.

And we shall ascribe to Thee praise, glory, thanksgiving, and adoration, now, always, and for ever and ever.

He signs himself with the sign of the cross, and they respond:—

Amen.

X. And he proceeds:—

Peace be with you:

They respond:—

With thee and with thy spirit.

And they give the (kiss of) peace to each other, and say:—

For all:
The Deacon says:—
Let us thank, entreat, and beseech.
The Priest says this prayer in secret:—
O Lord, mighty God, help my weakness through Thy clemency and the aid of Thy grace; and make me worthy of offering before Thee this oblation, as for the common aid of all, and to the praise of Thy Trinity, O Father, Son, and Holy Ghost.
Another prayer.

O our Lord and God, restrain our thoughts, that they wander not amid the vanities of this world. O Lord our God, grant that I may be united to the affection of Thy love, unworthy though I be. Glory be to Thee, O Christ.

Ascend into the chamber of Thy renowned light, O Lord; sow in me the good seed of humility; and under the wings of Thy grace hide me through Thy mercy. If Thou wert to mark iniquities, O Lord, who shall stand? Because there is mercy with Thee.

[The Priest says the following prayer in secret:—
O mother of our Lord Jesus Christ, beseech for me the only-begotten Son, who was born of thee, to forgive me my offences and my sins, and to accept from my feeble and sinful hands this sacrifice which my weakness offers upon this altar, through thy intercession for me, O holy mother.]

XI. When the Deacon shall say, With watchfulness and care, etc., immediately the Priest rises up and uncovers the sacraments, taking away the veil with which they were covered: he blesses the incense, and says a canon with a loud voice:—

The grace of our Lord Jesus Christ, and the love of God the Father, and the communion of the Holy Ghost, be with us all, now, etc.

He signs the sacraments, and they respond:—

Amen.

The Priest proceeds:—

Lift up your minds:

They respond:—

They are towards Thee, O God of Abraham, Isaac, and Israel, O glorious King.

The Priest.

The oblation is offered to God, the Lord of all.

They respond:—

It is meet and right.

The Deacon.

Peace be with you.

The Priest puts on the incense, and says this prayer:—

O Lord, Lord, grant me an open countenance before Thee, that with the confidence which is from Thee we may fulfil this awful and divine sacrifice with consciences free from all iniquity and bitterness. Sow in us, O Lord, affection, peace, and concord towards each other, and toward everyone.

And standing, he says in secret:—

Worthy of glory from every mouth, and of thanksgiving from all tongues, and of adoration and exaltation from all creatures, is the adorable and glorious name of Father, Son, and Holy Ghost, who created the world through His grace, and its inhabitants through His clemency, who saved men through His mercy, and showed great favor towards mortals. Thy majesty, O

Lord, thousands of thousands of heavenly *spirits*, and ten thousand myriads of holy angels, hosts of spirits, ministers of fire and spirit, bless and adore; with the holy cherubim and the spiritual seraphim they sanctify and celebrate Thy name, crying and praising, without ceasing crying unto each other.

They say with a loud voice:—

Holy, holy, holy, Lord God Almighty; full are the heavens and the earth of His glory.

The Priest in secret:—

Holy, holy, holy art Thou, O Lord God Almighty; the heavens and the earth are full of His glory and the nature of His essence, as they are glorious with the honor of His splendor; *as it is written*, The heaven and the earth are full of me, says the mighty Lord.

Holy art Thou, O God *our* Father, truly the only one, of whom the whole family in heaven and earth is named. Holy art Thou, Eternal Son, through whom all things were made.

Holy art Thou, Holy, Eternal Spirit, through whom all things are sanctified.

Woe to me, woe to me, who have been astonied, because I am a man of polluted lips, and dwell among a people of polluted lips, and my eyes have seen the King, the mighty Lord.

How terrible to-day is this place! For this is none other than the house of God and the gate of heaven; because Thou hast been seen eye to eye, O Lord.

Now, I pray, may Thy grace be with us, O Lord; purge away our impurities, and sanctify our lips; unite the voices of our insignificance with the sanctification of seraphim and archangels. Glory be to Thy tender mercies, because Thou hast associated the earthly with the heavenly.

And he proceeds, saying in secret this prayer, in a bowing posture:—

XII. And with those heavenly powers we give Thee thanks, even we, Thine insignificant, pithless, and feeble servants; because Thou hast granted unto us Thy great grace which cannot be repaid. For indeed Thou didst take upon Thee our human nature, that Thou mightest bestow life on us through Thy divinity; Thou didst exalt our low condition; Thou didst raise our ruined state; Thou didst rouse up our mortality; Thou didst wash away our sins; Thou didst blot out the guilt of our sins; Thou didst enlighten our intelligence, and Thou didst condemn our enemy, O Lord our God; and Thou didst cause the insignificance of our pithless nature to triumph.

Here follow the words of institution, after which:—

Through the tender mercies of Thy grace poured out, O clement One, pardon our offences and sins; blot out my offences in the judgment. And on account of all Thy aids and

Thy favors to us, we shall ascribe unto Thee praise, honor, thanksgiving, and adoration, now, always, and for ever and ever.

The Priest signs the sacraments. The response is made.

Amen.

The Deacon.

In your minds. Pray for peace with us.

The Priest says this prayer bowing, and in a low voice:—

O Lord God Almighty, accept this oblation for the whole Holy Catholic Church, and for all the pious and righteous fathers who have been pleasing to Thee, and for all the prophets and apostles, and for all the martyrs and confessors, and for all that mourn, that are in straits, and are sick, and for all that are under difficulties and trials, and for all the weak and the oppressed, and for all the dead that have gone from amongst us; then for all that ask a prayer from our weakness, and for me, a degraded and feeble sinner. O Lord our

God, according to Thy mercies and the multitude of Thy favors, look upon Thy people, and on me, a feeble man, not according to my sins and my follies, but that they may become worthy of the forgiveness of their sins through this holy body, which they receive with faith, through the grace of Thy mercy for ever and ever. Amen.

The Priest says this prayer of inclination in secret:—

XIII. Do Thou, O Lord, through Thy many and ineffable mercies, make the memorial good and acceptable *with that of* all the pious and righteous fathers who have been pleading before Thee in the commemoration of the body and blood of Thy Christ, which we offer to Thee upon Thy pure and holy altar, as Thou hast taught us; and grant unto us

Thy rest all the days of this life.

He proceeds with the Great Oblation:—

O Lord our God, bestow on us Thy rest and peace all the days of this life, that all the inhabitants of the earth may know Thee, that Thou art the only true God the Father, and

Thou didst send our Lord Jesus Christ, Thy Son and Thy beloved; and He Himself our Lord and God came

and taught us all purity and holiness. Make remembrance of prophets, apostles, martyrs, confessors, bishops, doctors, priests, deacons, and all the sons of the Holy
Catholic Church who have been signed with the sign of life, of holy baptism. We also, O
Lord:
He proceeds:—
We, Thy degraded, weak, and feeble servants who are congregated in Thy name, and now stand before Thee, and have received with joy the form which is from Thee, praising, glorifying, and exalting, commemorate and celebrate this great, awful, holy, and divine mystery of the passion, death, burial, and resurrection of our Lord and Savior Jesus Christ.
And may Thy Holy Spirit come, O Lord, and rest upon this oblation of Thy servants which they offer, and bless and sanctify it; and may it be unto us, O Lord, for the propitiation of our offences and the forgiveness of our sins, and for a grand hope of resurrection from the dead, and for a new life in the kingdom of the heavens, with all who have been pleasing before Him. And on account of the whole of Thy wonderful dispensation towards us, we shall render thanks unto Thee, and glorify Thee without ceasing in Thy Church, redeemed by the precious blood of Thy Christ, with open mouths and joyful countenances:
Canon.
Ascribing praise, honor, thanksgiving, and adoration to Thy holy, loving, and life-giving name, now, always, and forever.
The Priest signs the mysteries with the cross, and they respond:—
Amen.

The Priest bows himself and kisses the altar, first in the middle, then at the two sides right and left, and says this prayer:—

Have mercy upon me, O God, *down to the words*, and sinners shall be converted unto Thee: *and* unto Thee lift I up mine eyes, *down to* have mercy upon us, O Lord, have mercy upon us. *Also* stretch forth Thy hand, and let Thy right hand save me, O Lord; may Thy mercies remain upon me, O Lord, forever, and despise not the works of Thy hands.

Then he says this prayer:—

XIV. O Christ, peace of those in heaven and great rest of those below, grant that Thy rest and peace may dwell in the four parts of the world, but especially in Thy Holy Catholic Church; grant that the priesthood with the government may have peace; cause wars to cease from the ends of the earth, and scatter the nations that delight in wars, that we may enjoy the blessing of living in tranquility and peace, in all temperance and fear of God. Spare the offences and sins of the dead, through Thy grace and mercies forever.

And to those who are around the altar he says:—

Bless, O Lord. Bless, O Lord.

And he puts on the incense with which he fumes himself, and says:—

Sweeten, O Lord our God, the unpleasing savor of our souls through the sweetness of Thy love, and through it cleanse me from the stains of my sin, and forgive me my offences and sins, whether known or unknown to me.

A second time he takes the incense with both hands, and censes the mysteries; presently he says:—

The clemency of Thy grace, O our Lord and God, gives us access to these renowned, holy, life-giving, and divine mysteries, unworthy though we be.

The Priest repeats these words once and again, and at each interval unites his hands over his breast in the form of a cross. He kisses the altar in the middle, and receives with both hands the upper oblation; and looking up, says:—

Praise be to Thy holy name, O Lord Jesus Christ, and adoration to Thy majesty, always and forever. Amen.

For He is the living and life-giving bread which cometh down from heaven, and giveth life to the whole world, of which they who eat die not; and they who receive it are saved by it, and do not see corruption, and live through it forever; and Thou art the antidote of our mortality, and the resurrection of our entire frame.

XV. * * *

XVI. Praise to Thy holy name, O Lord. (*As above.*)

The Priest kisses the host in the form of a cross; in such a way, however, that his lips do not touch it, but appear to kiss it; and he says:—

Glory to Thee, O Lord; glory to Thee, O Lord, on account of Thine unspeakable gift to us, forever.

Then he draws nigh to the fraction of the host, which he accomplishes with both his hands, saying:—

We draw nigh, O Lord, with true faith, and break with thanksgiving and sign through Thy mercy the body and blood of our Life-giver, Jesus Christ, in the name of the Father, Son, and Holy Ghost.

And, naming the Trinity, he breaks the host, which he holds in his hands, into two parts: and the one which is in his left hand he lays down on the disk; with the other, which he holds in his right hand, he signs the chalice, saying:—

The precious blood is signed with the holy body of our Lord Jesus Christ. In the name of the Father, and the Son, and the Holy Ghost forever.

And they respond:—

Amen.

Then he dips it even to the middle in the chalice, and signs with it the body which is in the paten, saying:—

The holy body is signed with the propitiatory blood of our Lord Jesus Christ. In the name of the Father, and of the Son, and of the Holy Ghost forever.

And they respond:—

Amen.

And he unites the two parts, the one with the other, saying:—

Divided, sanctified, completed, perfected, united, and commingled have been these renowned, holy, life-giving, and divine mysteries, the one with the other, in the adorable and glorious name of Thy glorious Trinity, O Father, Son, and Holy Ghost, that they may be to us, O Lord, for the propitiation of our offences and the forgiveness of our sins; also for the grand hope of a resurrection from the dead, and of a new life in the kingdom of the heavens, for us and for the Holy Church of Christ our Lord, here and in every place whatsoever, now and always, and forever.

XVII. *In the meantime he signs the host with his right thumb in the form of a cross from the lower part to the upper, and from the right to the left, and thus forms a slight fissure in it where it has been dipped in the blood. He puts a part of it into the chalice in the form of a cross:*

the lower part is placed towards the priest, the upper towards the chalice, so that the place of the fissure looks to the chalice. He bows, and rising, says:—

He signs himself with the sign of the cross on his forehead, and does the same to those standing round him.

The Deacons approach, and he signs each one of them on the forehead, saying:—

Christ accept thy ministry: Christ cause thy face to shine: Christ save thy life: Christ make thy youth to grow.

And they respond:—

Christ accept thy oblation.

XVIII. All return to their own place; and the Priest, after bowing, rises and says, in the tone of the Gospel:—

The grace of our Lord Jesus Christ, and the love of God the Father, and the communion of the Holy Ghost, be with us all.

The Priest signs himself, and lifts up his hand over his head, so that it should be in the air, and the people be partakers in the singing:—

The Deacon says:—

We all with fear, etc.

And at these words:—

He hath given to us His mysteries:

The Priest begins to break the body, and says:—

Be merciful, O Lord, through Thy clemency to the sins and follies of Thy servants, and sanctify our lips through Thy grace, that they may give the fruits of glory and praise to Thy divinity, with all Thy saints in Thy kingdom.

And, raising his voice, he says:—

And make us worthy, O Lord our God, to stand before Thee continually without stain, with pure heart, with open countenance, and with the confidence which is from Thee, mercifully granted to us: and let us all with one accord invoke Thee, and say thus: Our

Father, etc.

The People say:—

Our Father, etc.

The Priest.

O Lord God Almighty, O Lord and our good God, who art full of mercy, we beg Thee, O Lord our God, and beseech the clemency of Thy goodness; lead us not into temptation, but deliver and save us from the evil one and his hosts; because Thine is the kingdom, the power, the strength, the might, and the dominion in heaven and on earth, now and always.

He signs himself, and they respond:—

Amen.

XIX. And he proceeds:—

Peace be with you.

They respond:—

With thee and with thy spirit.

He proceeds:—

It is becoming that the holy things should be to the holy in perfection.

And they say:—

One Holy Father: one holy Son: one Holy Ghost. Glory be to the Father, and to the Son, and to the Holy Ghost, for ever and ever. Amen.

The Deacon.

Praise ye.

And they say the responsory. And when the Deacon comes to carry the chalice, he says:—

Let us pray for peace with us.
The Priest says:—
The grace of the Holy Ghost be with thee, with us, and with those who receive Him.
And he gives the chalice to the Deacon.
The Deacon says:—
Bless, O Lord.
The Priest.

The gift of the grace of our Life-giver and Lord Jesus Christ be completed, in mercies, with all.
And he signs the people with the cross. In the meantime the responsories are said.
Brethren, receive the body of the Son, cries the Church, and drink ye His chalice with faith in the house of His kingdom.
On feast-days.
Strengthen, O Lord, etc.
On the Lord's Day.
O Lord Jesus Christ, etc.
Daily.
The mysteries which we have received, etc.
The responsories being ended, the Deacon says:—
All therefore, etc.
And they respond:—
Glory be to Himself on account of His ineffable gift.
The Deacon.
Let us pray for peace with us.
The Priest at the middle of the altar says this prayer:—
XX. It is meet, O Lord, just and right in all days, times, and hours, to thank, adore, and praise the awful

name of Thy majesty, because Thou hast through Thy grace, O Lord, made us, mortal men possessing a frail nature, worthy to sanctify Thy name with the heavenly beings, and to become partakers of the mysteries of Thy gift, and to be delighted with the sweetness of Thy oracles. And voices of glory and thanksgiving we ever offer up to Thy sublime divinity, O Lord.

Another.

Christ, our God, Lord, King, Savior, and Life-giver, through His grace has made us worthy to receive His body and His precious and all-sanctifying blood. May He grant unto us that we may be pleasing unto Him in our words, works, thoughts, and deeds, so that that pledge which we have received may be to us for the pardon of our offences, the forgiveness of our sins, and the grand hope of a resurrection from the dead, and a new and true life in the kingdom of the heavens, with all who have been pleasing before Him, through His grace and His mercies forever.

On ordinary days.

Praise, O Lord, honor, blessing, and thanksgiving we ought to ascribe to Thy glorious Trinity for the gift of Thy holy mysteries, which Thou hast given to us for the propitiation of our offences, O Lord of all.

Another.

Blessed be Thy adorable honor, from Thy glorious place, O Christ, the propitiator of our offences and our sins, and who takes away our follies through Thy renowned, holy, life-giving, and divine mysteries. Christ the hope of our nature always and forever. Amen.

Obsignation or final benediction.

May our Lord Jesus Christ, to whom we have ministered, and whom we have seen and honored in His renowned, holy, life-giving, and divine mysteries, Himself render us worthy of the splendid glory of His kingdom, and of gladness with His holy angels, and for confidence before Him, that we may stand at His right hand.

And on our entire congregation may His mercies and compassion be continually poured out, now and always, and ever.

On the Lord's Day and on feast-days.

May He Himself who blessed us with all spiritual blessings in the heavens, through Jesus Christ our Lord, and prepared us for His kingdom, and called us to the desirable good things which neither cease nor perish, as He promised to us in His life-giving Gospel, and said to the blessed congregation of His disciples—Verily, verily I say unto you, that everyone who eats my body and drinks my blood, abides in me, and I in him, and I will raise him up at the last day; and he cometh not to judgment, but I will make him pass from death to eternal life:

May He Himself now bless this congregation, and maintain our position, and render glorious our people who have come and rejoiced in receiving His renowned, holy, life-giving, and divine mysteries; and may ye be sealed and guarded by the holy sign of the Lord's cross from all evils, secret and open, now and always.

ELUCIDATIONS.

I.

(Disciple of the holy Peter, p. 551.)

The early use of the originals of this liturgy in the Alexandrian patriarchate accounts for its bearing the name of St. Mark,—"sister's son to Barnabas," as St. Paul calls him. That he was St. Peter's pupil may be inferred from that Apostle's language,—"Marcus, my son." See Clement's testimony concerning him (with Eusebius) in vol. ii. pp. 579, 580, this series. That he founded the "Evangelical See," though resting on great historic authority, seems to be doubted in our times by some.

II.

(Our holy father Mark, p. 556.)

While St. Mark could not have written this, it may, of course, have been added at a very early date. This most touching prayer bears marks of great antiquity, the reference to our "Christ-loving sovereign" comporting better with the early enthusiasm inspired by Constantine's conversion than with the disappointments incurred under his Arianizing or apostate successors. Now, this commemoration of St. Mark would of itself attach his name to the liturgy.

But here is the place to note the principles of these primitive prayers for saints departed. (1) They could only be offered in behalf of the holy dead who had fallen asleep in full communion with Christ and His Church; (2) They were not prayers for their deliverance out of one place into another; (3) They recognized the *repose* (not yet the *triumph*) of the faithful departed as incomplete, and hence (4) invoked for them a blessed consummation of peace and joy in the resurrection.

Now, all this is fatal to the Roman dogmas and usages, because (1) they thus include St. Mark and the Blessed Virgin in these commemorations; while Rome teaches, not only that these great saints went immediately to the excellent glory, and there have reigned with Christ ever since they died, but (2) that on this very ground, and that of their *supererogatory* merits, the Pontiff holds a purse of their excessive righteousness to dispense to meaner Christians.

St. Augustine speaks of his dear Nebridius as in Abraham's bosom, but finds comfort in commemorating him and Monica his mother, "because it is so comfortable." This is his idea, in a word: "Et credo jam feceris quod te rogo, sed (Ps. cxix. 108) *voluntaria* oris mei, approba, Domine."

III.

(Holy things for the holy, p. 559.)

Bingham has so fully elucidated this by quotations from Chrysostom (Hom. vii.) and others, that one might think it useless to attach to it any other meaning than that which Chrysostom understands in it; viz., "Holy things for holy persons." It occurs just before the communicating of the faithful, and has nothing whatever to do with the "elevation of the host,"—a Western ceremony of the fourteenth century. Yet, in an otherwise (generally) useful manual of liturgies, an attempt is made to give it this meaning; and the preceding prayer of "Intense Adoration," addressed to the Great High Priest in the heavens, is debased to eke out the weak idea. Nothing could be more averse to the primitive principle of worship; but it is sufficient to note the fact that the "elevation of the host" revolutionized the Eucharistic worship of the West as soon as it was established. (1) It abolished the Eucharist practically as the synaxis, or communion of the faithful, and made it only a sacrifice *for* them in their behalf; (2) not to be eaten and received, but to be gazed at; (3) not for all the faithful at all times, excluding even catechumens from beholding it, but to be displayed to all eyes in pompous ceremonials, carried through the streets, and dispensed only in half communion, once a year, to the individual communicant. All these ancient liturgies, corrupted as they are in all the mss. we possess, are yet liturgies for communicating the faithful, in their turns, one and all; and, so far, they are true to the Scriptures and the precepts of Christ and His Apostles. But well does the pious Hirscher exclaim, with reference to the Mass, as he was obliged to celebrate it in his own gorgeous cathedral at Freiburg in the Breisgau: "What would an Apostle think we were doing, should he enter during our ceremonies?" Also, "I know all that can be said in their favor. I know just as well that by them *the spirit is turned apart from internal godliness*, and borne away; and that, with such appeals to sense, withdrawal from things of sense becomes impossible....God is a Spirit: He looks to be adored *in spirit and in truth*, and all ceremonial which dulls the adoration of the spirit is odious to God. To glorify self, as His minister, before the King of kings, before the majesty of the Creator, before His Christ, naked and crucified,—is it not an absurdity, a ceremony of contradictions? The people no longer comprehend the ceremonial...to see them satisfied by mere corporal attendance, is it not deplorable? They do not understand Latin. Is it not melancholy that they take no real part in the touching offices of the Holy Week? Is not a deplorable indifference the result; in France, for example? Nay, at Rome also?"

His remonstrances were vain; he was cruelly censured, yet he died in the Papal communion. Dear Hirscher! The venerable man kissed me when I parted from him in 1851, and gave me his blessing with a primitive spirit of Christian charity. I gratefully quote him here.

In Germany a passing stranger often sees the pious peasantry at Mass, singing with all their hearts their beautiful German hymns. It misleads, however. They are not attending to the Mass, but consoling themselves by spiritual songs, while it goes on without their assistance. The bell rings: they adore the host, but that is all their relation to the worship of the Christian liturgies. Hirscher loved their hymns, but bewailed the utter loss of their liturgic communion, once common to the faithful.

IV.

(Teachers of the Easterns, etc., p. 561.)

The apostle Thaddeus is called *Addai* in Syriac. Maris is said to have been one of the seventy disciples, but his name is not on the list ascribed to Hippolytus. He was the first bishop of the people now called "Nestorians," but whom Dr. Badger prefers to call "the Christians of Assyria."

We have this liturgy in another form in Dr. Badger's important work, *Nestorians and their Rituals*. He selects that called "the Liturgy of Nestorius" from three which are in use among the Assyrians, but criticizes the translation of Renaudot as not entirely faultless. It is selected by Dr. Badger because of its reputed Nestorianism; while Hammond gives us what is here translated, in Renaudot's Latin. We must bear in mind, that, since the Ephesine Council (a.d. 431), these Christians have been separated from the communion of Eastern orthodoxy.

The Malabar Liturgy should be carefully compared with this by the student. A convenient translation of it is to be found in Neale and Littledale. A most important fact, by the way, is noted in their translation; viz., that in this Malabar "the invocation of the Holy Ghost, *contrary to the use of every other Oriental liturgy*, preceded the words of institution;" that is to say, in the work of *the Portuguese revisers*, a work from which Dr. Neale and his colleague feel justified in making "a considerable alteration" as to the order of the prayers.

The words of institution are found in the Malabar, and suggest that they belong not less to this Liturgy of the Assyrians, though, *ex summa verecundia*, they are omitted from the transcript, as the Lord's Prayer is omitted in the Clementine.

The normal form of this corrupted liturgy is credited with extreme antiquity by Dr. Neale. To his learned and cogent reasoning on the subject the student should by all means refer.

V.

(For all the prophets and confessors, p. 565.)

These commemorations of the dead, it will be noted, are in behalf of the most glorious apostles and saints, and for martyrs who go straight to glory. Obviously, as Usher has said, for whatever purpose, then, the departed were commemorated, it was not to change their estate before the resurrection, much less to relieve them from purgatorial penalties. This comes out in the "Liturgy of St. Chrysostom" (so called), where it is said: "We offer to Thee this reasonable service for those who have fallen asleep in faith,...patriarchs, apostles, evangelists, martyrs,...and every *just one made perfect in the faith: especially* our all-holy, undefiled, most blessed Lady, *Theotokos* and ever-virgin Mary," etc. But she, they tell us, was *assumed* into glory, like Christ Himself, and reigns with Him as "Queen of Angels," etc.

See Elucidation II. p. 569.

VI.

(The propitiatory blood, etc., p. 566.)

The peril of confounding the early use of this idea of propitiation with the mediæval theory, which is quite another, is well pointed out and enforced by Burbidge. The primitive writers and the ancient liturgies "do not regard the Eucharist as being *itself* a propitiatory offering," but it is the perpetual pleading of the blood of propitiation once offered. Thus St. Chrysostom: "We do not offer another sacrifice, but *always the same*." So far, his words might be quoted to favor the Middle-Age doctrine; but he guards himself, and adds: "or, *rather, we make a memorial* of the sacrifice."

The rhetoric of the liturgies and of the Fathers was unhappily made into the logic of the Schoolmen, and hence the stupendous system of propitiatory Masses, with Masses for the dead, and that traffic in Masses which so fearfully defiles the priesthood of Western Europe and the Spanish and Portuguese colonies in America. In vain does the pious Hirscher complain: "The rich, then, are the happy sinners in this respect: they can buy innumerable Masses, and establish them in perpetuity; their privileges have no limit, and their advantages over the poor extend through all eternity." His book was put into the Index (Acts xvi. 19, xix. 27), but it was never answered.

VII.

Let me now recur to Elucidation III. on p. 507, to which I would here add the following from Bishop Williams, as there quoted:—

"In both the Mozarabic and the Gallican Liturgies there was an invocation as well as an oblation. Irenæus says (and he, writing at Lyons, must have in mind the Gallican Liturgy), 'The bread which is of the earth, having received the *invocation of God*, is no longer common bread, but the Eucharist.' The word translated 'invocation' is ἐπίκλησιν; and it is worthy of notice that Basil and Cyril of Jerusalem use the same word in evidently the same technical sense (Harvey's *Irenæus*, vol. ii. pp. 205–207 and notes). In another passage Irenæus speaks even more distinctly: 'We offer to God the bread and the cup of blessing, giving thanks to Him for that He hath commanded the earth to bring forth these fruits for our nourishment; and, having finished the offering, we invoke the Holy Spirit that He may exhibit (or declare, ἀποφήνῃ) this sacrifice and bread the body of Christ, and the cup the blood of Christ, that they who shall receive these antitypes may obtain remission of sins and everlasting life' (Harvey's *Irenæus*, vol. ii. p. 502). This passage is a remarkable one. It proves beyond question, that, in the time of Irenæus (*d.* a.d. 202 or 208), the Liturgy of Gaul contained an invocation of the Holy Ghost following the oblation of the bread and cup.

Moreover, when we compare the words of Irenæus with those of the Clementine Liturgy, their agreement is too clear and precise to be explained as a mere chance-matter. The liturgy reads, 'Send down Thy Holy Spirit on this sacrifice, the witness of the sufferings of the Lord Jesus, that He may exhibit (ἀποφήνῃ) this bread, the body of Thy Christ, and this cup, the blood of Thy Christ, that they who shall receive,' etc. Irenæus says as above, using the same word (ἀποφήνῃ), a word which is found, it is believed, in no liturgy but the Clementine."

Now I humbly suggest that Justin Martyr and Irenæus *concur* in giving us evidence that the *Clementine Liturgy* is substantially that which was used in Rome and Gaul in their times. The latter may have received it from Polycarp. The use of the Roman and the Greek churches was uniform in his day, as may be inferred from the intercourse of Polycarp and Victor.

**Find this and other great works of the
Early Church Fathers at
lighthousechristianpublishing.com.**

Our Father who art in heaven, hallowed be thy name.
Thy kingdom come, Thy will be done, on earth as it is in heaven.
Give us this day our daily bread and forgive us our trespasses as we forgive those who trespass against us.
And lead us not into temptation, but deliver us from evil, for Thine is the kingdom, the power and the glory. Forever and ever.

Amen

Hail Mary full of grace, the Lord is with thee. Blessed art thou amongst women and blessed is the fruit of thy womb Jesus. Holy Mary mother of God, pray for us sinners, now and the hour of our death.

www.ingramcontent.com/pod-product-compliance
Lightning Source LLC
Chambersburg PA
CBHW050225100526
44585CB00017BA/2013